The Piñon Pine:
A Natural and
Cultural History

The Piñon Pine

A Natural and Cultural History

Ronald M. Lanner

With a Section on Pine-Nut Cookery by
Harriette Lanner

University of Nevada Press

Reno · Las Vegas

University of Nevada Press, Reno, Nevada 89557 USA
Book design by Dave Comstock
Cover design by Carrie House
Printed in the United States of America

Library of Congress Cataloging in Publication Data
Lanner, Ronald M.
The piñion pine.
Bibliography: p.
Includes index.
1. Pinyon pines—Southwest, New. 2. Cookery (Pine nuts) 3. Indians of
North America—Southwest, New—Food. 4. Indians of North America—
Southwest, New—Religion and mythology. I. Title.
QK494.5.P66L36   1981   585'.2   81-119
ISBN: 978-0-87417-066-5 (pbk.:alk. paper)   AACR2

Portions of chapter 12 have previously appeared in *Desert Magazine*
(April, 1978) and are used by permission of that publication.

Material quoted on pave v is from *Rabbit Boss* by Thomas Sanchez.
© 1973 Alfred A. Knopf, Inc., New York. Used by permission of the
publisher.

Material quoted on page 66 is from *The Pueblo of Jemez* by Elsie Clews
Parsons. © 1925 Yale University Press. Used by permission of the publisher.

Material quoted on page 78 is from *Karnee* by Lalla Scott. © 1966
University of Nevada Press. Used by permission of the publisher.

This book has been reproduced as a digital reprint.

To Nicholas T. Mirov
(1893–1980)
whose love affair with pines
was so long an inspiration
and an example
and
to Numaga of the Paiutes
who knew what a
tree was worth

The green time was golden and brown.
The waters ran clear. The Sun held long
on the people coming together from
across the land. Coming up from the
mountains. Up from the hotlands. Up
from the valleys. Joining hands for the
Big Time among the groves of the Sacred
Tree, the Piñon. Singing up Gumsaba.

Thomas Sanchez, *Rabbit Boss*

Contents

Preface and Acknowledgments

Man, impressed by power, judges trees by their size. We name our giant Sequoias after generals and praise our redwoods, firs, and tall pines as stately or majestic. Foresters, as though reassured to find our profligacy reflected in nature's mirror, marvel at fast-growing eucalypts and poplars which, in their short lives, consume enormous quantities of water and nutrients.

Trees that live more modestly and that do not attain great heights are thought poor and humble, objects of pity. The piñon pine, "a broad tree with a round head, similar in size and form, but not in ramification, to the cultivated Apple-tree," is regarded as lowly, a pygmy, a dwarf, a scrub conifer. And while the clear-cutting of forest pines in Wyoming and Montana became an environmental *cause célèbre*, the wholesale bulldozing of little desert pines in the Southwest went on for years almost unnoticed.

But a tree is what you make of it, and once, much was made of the piñon. This little tree produced the fuel, building materials, food, and medicines that enabled prehistoric Indians to establish their cultures on the Colorado

Plateau—and to survive into the present as Hopi, Zuñi, Pueblo, and Navajo. It was the piñon that made the Great Basin the coarse-grained Eden of the pine-nut eaters who picked their winter sustenance from the treetops: the Washo, the Shoshones, the Paiutes. Piñon served early whites with equal generosity, and the roster of mounted pine-nut eaters reads like a roll call of western American exploration: Cabeza de Vaca, Coronado, Tovar, Espejo, Escalante, Frémont, the Army of the West, the Donner party.

Most Americans have seen piñon pines countless times on the screens of movie theaters and television sets. Hollywood's stagecoaches have been ambushed in piñon country, villains have been headed off at passes through ranges black with piñon, and many victims of bloody skirmishes have recovered from their Apache-inflicted wounds in the shade of a sprawling desert pine.

And for once, the casting is to Hollywood's credit. There are, indeed, piñon pines in bullet-scarred Apache Pass through the Dos Cabezas, and in Utah's Lookout Pass, where Pony Express riders rode up from Skull Valley, slapping leather on the way to Salt Lake City. And on the Big Ridge that Butch Cassidy crossed, heading into Robber's Roost above the Dirty Devil, those short-needled pines he zig-zagged through were piñons.

Piñon country, where these pines grow, is sprawling country. It stretches from trans-Pecos Texas to the Santa Ynez Mountains of Southern California, and from the south of Idaho deep into Mexico. It lies between the deserts and the high places. Going from desert basin to snowy peak, the first conifers you find are usually scattered junipers. This is the beginning of the woodland, a vegetation community dominated by scattered trees of low stature, a transition zone between desert scrub and mountain forest. Go higher, where the junipers thicken, and round-crowned pines will be mingling with them. Higher still, where the hillsides and mesa tops are black and woolly in the twilight, where a man on foot cannot walk a straight line for the trees blocking his way, or erect for the eye-poking needles, and you are in dense piñon-juniper woodland. Follow the slope further, and taller trees—usually ponderosa pines and Douglas-firs—begin to replace the woodland trees. Only then have you left the woodland and entered the forest.

Many visitors to the Southwest have seen the little pines, where they are a feature of most of the national parks, monuments, and forests. The piñon-juniper woodland can be found at Capitol Reef, Grand Canyon, Mesa Verde, Canyonlands, Zion, Arches, Bryce Canyon, and Big Bend national parks. Among the national monuments of piñon country are Gila Cliff Dwellings, Dinosaur, Lehman Caves, Chiricahua, Natural Bridges, and Navaho. People who live in the Southwest know the piñon pine well. Many of them still eat its nuts in the fall, and New Mexicans still burn its wood in *candelarias*, Christmas campfires that hark back to Spanish days.

Yet, the fact that pines grow at all on millions of acres of semidesert land in the Southwest and Mexico startles many, whose stereotype of the pine seems to stem from the Song of Hiawatha. But Hiawatha's western brothers, who breathed the clear dry air of "arid slopes and tablelands," wove these little desert trees intimately into the fabric of their lives, and in so doing, they transformed the piñon pine from a fascinating biological curiosity to an organism of the deepest cultural and historic significance. This book is about those trees.

Our story traces a wavy line through time: geological, prehistoric, historic, and current. It begins long before any but the most far-sighted Creator ever thought of making warm-blooded bipeds, and it continues through the arrival of those bipeds in piñon country—Paleo-Indians, the Indians of recorded history, Spaniards, and Anglo-Americans. It documents a changing relationship between man and woodland, from one in which man's fate was determined by the bounty of the ecosystem to one in which man modifies, even destroys, that ecosystem for immediate profit.

No tree is a simple thing, and least of all one with so many links to our own species. Every tree, like every other living organism, is at the center of its own four-dimensional spider web: tug on this strand or that and see what quivers, what falls, what comes in or goes out, what lives or dies, what grows fat—and when.

The silks we tug will lead to Australia, to the Andes, to Mexico, and to Siberia. Soldiers will fall out, as will charcoal makers, ranchers and mountain men, medicine men, scientists, bean farmers, miners, a few villains, and a hero or two. All these we will meet in the pages that follow, and more.

*   *   *

The research that led to this book would not have been possible without the help of many of my students, friends, and associates during the past decade. Among my former students I would especially like to thank Ron Warnick, Norman Channing, David Van Den Berg, Earl Hutchison, Elizabeth Meyn, Michael Jenkins, and James Bryan. Stanley Paher of Las Vegas, Nevada, made fruitful suggestions for unearthing data on the Nevada charcoal industry of the nineteenth century, and Philip Torchio of Utah State University directed me to some fascinating entomological literature. Professional associates who helped me understand something of their own crafts were Dr. Thomas VanDevender, University of Arizona; Dr. David Hurst Thomas, American Museum of Natural History; Dr. J. Wayne Brewer, Colorado State University; and Dr. Steven B. Vander Wall of Utah State University. Dr. Austin Fife of Utah State University drew my attention to Indian folklore regarding the piñon tree. I would also like to thank David Hurst Thomas for allowing me to examine piñon macrofossils from Gatecliff Shelter and to cite them in the text. Dr. John Andresen of the University of Toronto provided details of his visit to the piñons of Cerro Potosí. Harriette, David, and Deborah Lanner gave invaluable assistance on many field trips in the Southwestern states and Mexico. Many thanks to Gladys and Saggie Williams for insights on piñon as viewed by Great Basin Indians, and to Flanigan's Old Prints of Logan, Utah, for botanical illustrations. Finally, I would like to thank my typist, Joyce Bedford, for her patience and precision.

Logan, Utah   RONALD M. LANNER
December 1980

CHAPTER 1

Woodlands of Piñon Country

O ver seventy-five thousand square miles of southwestern United States landscape is dominated by a woodland community consisting mainly of pines and junipers. As one travels across this area the species change, but the overall physiognomy of the community remains the same. This is the piñon-juniper woodland, an open forest of low, round-crowned trees, often bushy or contorted. It is the characteristic vegetation type of the southern Rocky Mountain foothills, the mesas of the Colorado Plateau, and the mountains of the Great Basin. On favorable sites and where past mismanagement of the land has not been severe, the woodland forms a dense cover and the trees reach thirty to forty feet in height or more. On drier sites near the desert margin, spacing widens and tree size diminshes.*

The pines and junipers that define this far-ranging plant community have left their names scattered on the maps of half a dozen states: Juniper, Cedar (for juniper) City, Cedar Creek, Cedar Fort, Cedarview, Cedar Crest,

*Bibliographic sources are cited in the notes following the text.

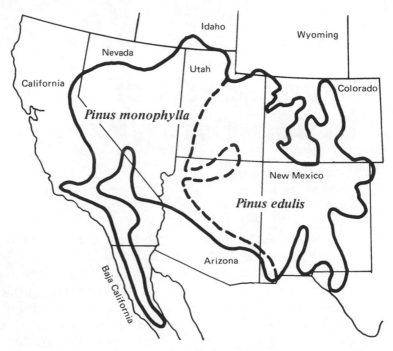

Generalized distribution map showing range of singleleaf piñon
(Pinus monophylla) west of the dashed line and Colorado piñon
(Pinus edulis) to the east. At many points along the dashed line
both species occur together and hybridize.

Cedar Breaks, Cedarvale, Cedro, Cedarhill, Cedar Mountain, Cedar Springs, Pine Nut Mountains, Pine Grove
Hills, Pine Valley, Piñon, Pine Grove Mine, Pinyon Flat,
Pine Mountain Summit, Piñon Hills, and many other
variations.

Pines are cone-bearing evergreen trees whose needles
are clustered in bundles or fascicles attached to the shoots.
There are usually two, three, or five needles per fascicle,

but sometimes more, depending on the species. The needles are bound together at the base by the fascicle or bundle sheath, which consists of the remains of the numerous scales that took shape just before the needles were formed; in many species, including the piñons, the sheath soon disintegrates. One of the piñon pines, of which more will be said later, is exceptional in that it has single needles within its fascicles.

Pines have woody seed cones made up of cone scales arranged in spirals around a central axis. The seeds are borne on the upper surface of the cone scales. While the seeds of most species have membranous wings, those of piñon pines and of a number of other species are unwinged. The membranous wing allows most pines to disseminate their seeds widely on the wind, but the piñons lack this ability.

There are approximately a hundred pine species. About a third of these, among them the piñons, are classified as *soft pines,* largely on the basis of wood and leaf anatomy. The wood of the soft pines is usually soft, even-textured, and creamy white. Their summerwood is light in color, making it difficult to count their annual rings with accuracy. The best-known soft pines of North America are the eastern and western white pines, and the sugar pine of California.

Eleven species of soft pine make up the group known variously as the piñon, pinyon, or North American nut pines. "Pinyon" is to piñon as "canyon" is to cañon. It is the anglicized version of the Spanish *piñón,* for the edible seeds of these desert conifers. The trees are, in Spanish, *pinos piñoneros,* or nut-bearing pines.

Following is an introduction to the eleven species of piñon pine.

1. Singleleaf piñon (*Pinus monophylla* Torr. & Frém.) is the piñon pine of the Great Basin and Mohave Desert borderlands. Small fragmented populations are also found

Mature singleleaf piñon in the Great Basin, Nevada. (Photo by U.S. Forest Service, Intermountain Region)

in a belt across Arizona into southwestern New Mexico. It is common in Nevada and in parts of southern California and western Utah. There are several populations in Baja California, the southernmost in the Sierra de Asamblea, about three hundred miles south of the Mexican border. Its single leaf is unique among the pines of the world. It will often be referred to in this book as *"monophylla."*

2. **Colorado piñon** (*Pinus edulis* Engelm.) is a familiar producer of commercial pine nuts. This species is well known to residents of Colorado, New Mexico, Arizona, and eastern Utah, where it forms vast woodlands on the

Mature Colorado piñon on Ashley National Forest, Utah. (Photo by U.S. Forest Service, Intermountain Region)

mesas and Rocky Mountain foothills. Its needles are mostly in bundles of two, but some trees also have many three-needled fascicles. We will often refer to it as *"edulis"* in this book, and much will be said about it.

* * *

The remaining nine piñons will be much less prominent in our story. They are briefly described here:

3. Mexican piñon (*Pinus cembroides* Zucc.), mainly Mexican in distribution, is found from northern Sonora and Chihuahua southward to the state of Puebla and near

Mexican piñon in foothills of the Sierra Madre Occidental,
Chihuahua, Mexico. (Photo by the author)

the southern tip of Baja California, but it also appears in
the Big Bend area of Texas. Mexican piñon is usually
three-needled. Its very thick-shelled nuts are sold in
Mexican markets.

In older literature the name *P. cembroides* was under-
stood to include the two species already described above.
They were considered for some years to be *P. cembroides*
var. *monophylla* and var. *edulis*. Modern taxonomists,
however, have tended to distinguish them as three separate species rather than as members of a single, extremely

variable species. In taxonomists' jargon, they are no longer "lumped," but have been "split."

4. **Border piñon** (*Pinus discolor* Bailey and Hawksworth) was originally described in 1968 as a variety of Mexican piñon but has recently been raised to specific rank. Its needles have contrasting blue green outer surfaces and whitish inner surfaces, and its cones are the smallest of the piñons. It grows in southern Arizona and New Mexico and adjacent northern Mexico. Southwestern tourists have seen it on Kitt Peak and in the Santa Catalinas outside Tucson.

5. **Texas piñon** (*Pinus remota* [Little] Bailey and Hawksworth) was described in 1966 as another variety of Mexican piñon, but it too is quite distinctive and has now been given the status of species. The thinnest-shelled of the piñons, it is mainly found in northeastern Mexico but is best known from west Texas where it occurs in scattered stands.

6. **Nelson piñon** (*Pinus nelsonii* Shaw) is a peculiar tree, notable for its long-stemmed cones and its needles that stick tightly together; it is narrowly distributed in Mexico. Little is known of it, but it is locally important as a nut producer, and local Indians prefer the flavor of its seeds to that of the Mexican piñon with which it is usually found.

7. **Pince piñon** (*Pinus pinceana* Gord.) is another little-known species of central Mexico with moderately long cones and needles.

8. **Potosí piñon** (*Pinus culminicola* Andresen & Beaman) is the five-needled inhabitant of a mountaintop in the Mexican state of Nuevo León and of some high ridges to the south. In form, it is more a large shrub than a tree and on the top of Cerro Potosí takes on the aspect of a contorted timberline conifer.

9. **Martínez piñon** (*Pinus maximartinezii* Rzedowski) is one of the newest of the piñon pines to science. This species, with long needles and inch-long nuts, grows in a

remote canyon in Mexico's state of Zacatecas and, according to local inhabitants, on some nearby hills. There are five needles in the fascicle, and the incredible cone—up to ten inches long and four pounds in weight when green—is one of the most bizarre products of any pine anywhere.

10. Sierra Juárez piñon (*Pinus juarezensis* Lanner) is a five-needled piñon of northern Baja California and extreme southern California. Formerly, this tree was considered a member of the species Parry piñon (*Pinus quadrifolia*). In my judgment most of the trees that were called Parry piñon are an assortment of hybrids resulting from interbreeding between Sierra Juárez piñon and singleleaf piñon. Therefore, I have described the five-needled form as a new species and demoted Parry piñon to hybrid status.

11. Johannis piñon (*Pinus johannis* Robert) is a dwarfish, three-needled species that grows on the high slopes of limestone mountains west of the ancient copper-mining center of Concepción del Oro in Zacatecas, Mexico. It was described for the first time in 1978.

While most of these piñons are known to form pure stands, usually they intermix with one or more juniper species, forming the association called "piñon-juniper woodland." The junipers are evergreen trees and shrubs that vary from prostrate forms to forest trees a hundred feet tall. Like the pines, they are classed as conifers, though their "cones" are small, fleshy, berrylike spheres sometimes less than a quarter-inch in diameter. There are about seventy species of juniper, ranging from the Arctic region to the equatorial highlands of East Africa and from sea level in the West Indies to over 12,000 feet in the Himalayas. Many of the world's junipers are associated with pines. In many parts of this country, junipers are commonly called cedars, but they are not true cedars in the botanical sense, as are, for example, the Lebanon cedars.

Juniper berries provide gin with its characteristic taste, as well as its name. Six juniper species are known to mingle with piñon pines in one place or another in the Southwest, but only three of these—alligator juniper, one-seed juniper, and Utah juniper—help to make up the extensive woodlands that often characterize the community.

Alligator juniper (*Juniperus deppeana* Steud.) is the largest representative of its genus in the Southwest, attaining heights of sixty feet, and diameters often over three feet. It is widespread in Mexico and reaches its northern limit in north-central Arizona and New Mexico. Alligator juniper is found in woodland with Colorado piñon, Mexican piñon, and with singleleaf piñon south of the Mogollon Rim in Arizona. These woodlands often contain one-seed juniper and several evergreen oak species as well. For example, in a singleleaf piñon stand in the Gila Mountains of Arizona, in which both alligator and one-seed junipers were present, there were also Emory oak, Arizona oak, Palmer oak, and shrub live oak.

One-seed juniper (*Juniperus monosperma* [Engelm.] Sarg.) extends from central Colorado to central Arizona, is widely distributed throughout most of New Mexico, and thence southwards into west Texas and Mexico. Though it sometimes attains considerable size, it is most often seen as a large shrub or a small tree, multistemmed and round crowned. At low elevations, and on sites too dry to support piñon, one-seed juniper is often found in pure open stands. It commonly grows in woodland with alligator juniper, and like that species it is associated with Colorado piñon and border piñon, and with singleleaf piñon in Arizona south of the Mogollon Rim.

Utah juniper (*J. osteosperma* [Torr.] Little) is the most important member of its genus found in the piñon-juniper woodland. In the Great Basin, singleleaf piñon is nearly always associated with it; at lower elevations where conditions are too arid for any pine, the Utah juni-

Utah juniper, a member of the cypress family that is usually associated with singleleaf and Colorado piñon. (Photo by the author)

per forms open, pure stands, even extending at times close to the edge of salt flats. On the Colorado Plateau, Utah juniper is the constant associate of the Colorado piñon, again forming pure stands where the pine cannot become established. It covers, consequently, vast acreages in northern Arizona, Utah, and Nevada.

CHAPTER 2

Through Time and Space

How Piñons Came to Piñon Country

Pines first appeared somewhere in northern Asia about 180 million years ago, in the Triassic Period of the Mesozoic Era. It was the Age of Reptiles, and early pines shaded reposing dinosaurs, provided perches for toothed birds, and stood mute while novel egg-laying mammals appeared and passed into oblivion. The fossil record shows that after about 75 million years pines had already differentiated into the two major types still found today—the hard pines and the soft pines. This divergence may have coincided with the southward and westward migration of pines into regions that were themselves rapidly changing. The Eurasian land mass was during this time the center of great uplifts that built the Alps and Himalayas upon a landscape which had earlier held great inland seas and swamps. The resulting diversity of habitats probably accelerated the evolution of new pine species. Eventually, there were pines for the seacoast, resistant to the salty bite of ocean spray, and pines for the cold lands of the north. There were pines for the dry rocky wastes of the interior and pines adapted to the steamy peninsular forests far to the south, in the thrall of the monsoon cycle.

Pines also migrated into North America, across the wide Bering land bridge that several times connected Alaska with Siberia. Some of these traversed North America in an easterly path, crossing land bridges to Greenland and Iceland, and thence to Europe. Others slowly made their way south along the upland bordering the western shore of the Cretaceous Epeiric Sea, a great body of water that bisected this continent from the Yukon to Texas. A number of pines followed this route as far as the highlands of Mexico and beyond.

Few areas in the world have been such a haven for pines as Mexico. Paleobotanists speak of Mexico as a secondary center of evolution for pines and numerous other plants. What they mean is that in the salubrious Mexican climates, among the rugged hills and high valleys, in wet lowlands and on stony slopes, there was a great burst of speciation. Under the enormously varied environmental conditions—there are places in Mexico where one can lose 11,000 feet of elevation in a twenty-five-mile drive— genetic variants that would elsewhere have perished were able to find an ecological niche in which to prosper. The result has been a confusing array of surviving pines that has challenged taxonomists for over a century. Mexico's pine flora is full of look-alike species that probably hybridize frequently, generating a wide assortment of variable progeny.

Among the pines that migrated into the Mexican highlands were some members of the soft pine group, the five-needled pines with soft, creamy wood and stately habit. Two such species still reside in mountain forests of central and southern Mexico. It seems likely that the piñon group evolved from a similar five-needled pine and that this sequence of events occurred in the Mexican highlands.

Although the evidence is indirect, it is fairly consistent with this hypothesis. The piñons have always been classified as soft pines, for good anatomical reasons. Most soft pines are five-needled, and so are several of the piñons *(culminicola, juarezensis, maximartinezii)*. Several of the piñons centered in Mexico occupy very small home ranges or consist of only a few isolated populations, which suggests that they are either relics of other times or new species getting underway *(culminicola, pinceana, nelsonii, maximartinezii, johannis)*. Such diversity of relicts is usually considered evidence of a center of great evolutionary activity.

Another feature suggesting the subtropical origin of piñons is the commonness of "summer shoots" in the group. These are portions of stems and branches that form and spontaneously elongate after the usual extension of the bud has been completed in the spring. Summer shoots are most common in pines of tropical and subtropical areas and become less common in areas of rigorous climate.

Last of all, it is now possible to explain how a white pine of the moist shady forest, with small seeds bearing long membranous wings to allow their dispersion in the wind, can give rise to stubby little pines of the arid hills, with their great wingless seeds. This explanation forms the subject of a later chapter, where we shall see how certain intelligent birds have been the architects of the piñon pine.

Sixty million years ago, during the Paleocene Epoch, the North American climate gradually began to grow warmer and drier. The great drought lasted 30 million years, well into the Oligocene, and during its long sway it worked changes in the vegetation. Only drought-hardy plants were able to survive the rigorous new climatic regime: many moisture-demanding species became extinct. An array of aggressive new forms, shaped by natural selection as the inheritors of a semiarid subcontinent, then invaded and occupied the ground, mainly during the Miocene. One of these species was the progenitor of the piñon pines. Its descendants would undergo many evolutionary changes over the ages and would produce the surviving species of piñons.

Of course, the evolving piñon pines did not exist in a vacuum; they had many plant and animal associates that were members of the same ecosystem and equal sharers in the challenge posed by the great drought. Consequently, an arid land *flora* evolved, termed by the American paleobotanist Axelrod the Madro-Tertiary Geoflora. The plants of this flora covered much of northern Mexico and the American Southwest, and included drought-hardy oaks, locust, mountain mahogany, and arbutus. The watercourses were fringed with massive sycamores, delicate willows, cottonwoods, and desert palms. And on the slopes grew a drought resistant piñon pine. The plant community was probably quite similar to that found today in the chaparral and woodland country of Arizona.

The northward migration was like an eddy in the great overall southward flow of pines in North America. It was a local phenomenon brought about by the presence, in Mexico, of an adaptable piñon pine stock that could take advantage of the opportunity afforded by climatic change.

By this time, the piñon pines bore little resemblance to their sylvan ancestors. They were no longer fast-growing trees able to compete for sunlight with other tall trees of the moist, shady forest. Natural selection had replaced that prototype with slow-growing, short-trunked models which used water sparingly. From a stock that had originated in moist forest, arid conditions had triggered the evolution of a pine adapted to hot, dry, subtropical conditions. The piñon migration to the north now required the adaptation of some of these pines to colder mountain

habitats. One important adjustment still had to be made
in the piñon's life rhythm.

On the hot Mexican *sierra,* pine growth occurs during
the spring and summer monsoon season. Early rains stimulate early growth and late rains delay growth. This is
essentially a subtropical growth rhythm, and as piñons
spread north into colder climates it became a serious lia-
bility. A tree that started to grow in July, for example, in
response to the late arrival of the rains, would still have
tender new shoots in September and would be vulnerable
to autumn frosts on the high mesas of Arizona, Colorado,
and New Mexico. This danger could be avoided if growth
began earlier, as soon as the danger from equally detri-
mental spring frosts was past. Thus, in the more northerly
areas where winters were more severe than those of Mexico, the piñon pines that grew best were those that started
growth early. Early growth was further encouraged by a
good supply of soil moisture deposited from melting winter snows, a crucial factor missing from the milder areas
to the south. So it is that the growth of northern piñon
pines is stimulated by rising temperatures. They generally
start their growth in May and become dormant long before the advent of cold weather.

Visualize a migrating population moving from a mild
area to one where winters were more severe. Over a period of many millenia those trees whose genetic endowment allowed them to cope with the new conditions lived
longer and reproduced more frequently. Eventually, their
offspring dominated the species' population in the new
area, while those less well adapted contributed little to
later generations and their genes were lost to posterity.

This process of natural selection, acting on the differen-
tial ability to fill the ranks of the next generation, is usually very gradual, with millions of years required for the
emergence of distinctive new species. But occasionally
evolution of a species is rapid, even abrupt; instead of
requiring the slow accumulation of small differences, it

comes about by the sudden appearance and fixation of a drastic mutation. Twenty million years ago, during the Miocene, such a random act of creation occurred in an ancestral *edulis* population, bringing into being the progenitor of the new species *monophylla*. In so doing, it altered the lifeway of men not yet evolved.

CHAPTER 3

Origin of a Species

How the Singleleaf Piñon was Born

The mutation of a gene is not a dramatic event. It is, in fact, a commonplace. According to one estimate of mutation frequency, an organism with the complex chromosomal apparatus of a pine has about a one-in-ten chance of bearing a mutant gene. It is further estimated that only about one in a thousand of these mutations is likely to be beneficial; most mutations merely disrupt the workings of the delicately balanced adaptive complex of genes that, in unison, carry on an organism's business. In their 180 million years, the pines seem to have made the best of their "genetic load" of mutations. Unlike many other plants whose evolution has come about largely by the multiplication and rearrangement of entire chromosomes, the pines seem to have evolved and differentiated by the accumulation of gene, or "point," mutations.

Mutations may be caused by such physical phenomena as cosmic radiation, ultraviolet radiation, or near-lethal high temperatures. Evidence is beginning to emerge that even some microorganisms are capable of producing substances that cause mutations in plants.

Whatever the cause may have been, the result was an altered chromosome in one of the cells in the mutated pine, and eventually the mutation appeared in the embryo of a germinating seed. In this way a mutant seedling was born.

The young mutant tree differed from the nonmutants. The altered molecular composition of its mutated gene modified certain of its biochemical processes. The tree responded by suppressing the development of one needle in each of its fascicles, allowing only one needle of each potential pair to appear. Thus, its needles were borne not in fascicles or bundles of two, but attached *singly* to the twig. The mutation probably caused other more subtle changes as well, for mutated genes usually have multiple effects, but the single-needle habit—"monophylly"—is of great interest to us because it clearly distinguishes the mutant from its two-needled progenitor.

The appearance of a mutant form in a population does not guarantee its long-term survival, even if the mutation is not lethal or harmful to the individual that bears it. A mutation of neutral value (if indeed there is such a thing as a totally innocuous alteration—and the point is controversial among population geneticists) will, according to genetic theory, be quickly "swamped" and eliminated. In order for a mutation to spread and become the standard model within a population, it must confer on its bearer so clearcut an advantage in the game of life that the average bearer consistently leaves behind more offspring than the average nonbearer.

Single-needled piñon pines did not replace the two-needled form in the Rockies or on the Colorado Plateau.

Instead they formed a new population that broke off from the home range of the parent and pioneered new areas to the west.

How might it have happened? Envision the first mutant tree standing on a rock-strewn mountainside among its two-needled brethren. After perhaps a century it starts to flower—producing each spring young ovule-bearing female cones and male cones filled with pale yellow, dust-like pollen. Some of its pollen grains fertilize its own ovules. The seeds resulting from this inbreeding eventually germinate, some becoming trees in which monophylly is firmly fixed. Within a few generations the local piñon pine population harbors many such one-needled trees.

Presently, some sort of habitat change comes about that favors survival and reproduction of the single-needled pines over the original two-needled stock. Perhaps a wider than usual swing of the environmental pendulum puts all the pines in the mutation area under stress, and by grace of their altered genetic endowment only the mutants survive, becoming the founders of a new race. The new race finds favorable conditions for its growth to the west and starts to colonize the heights overlooking the dry-summer deserts.

Geographic isolation soon prevents crossbreeding between the two races and accentuates their differences. At this point they may be regarded as distinct species.

This scenario, of course, can only be speculative; it is impossible to know with certainly how a wild species originated. Guidance in this matter is gratefully accepted from Sir Francis Bacon's *Sylva Sylvarum:*

> The transmutation of species is, in the vulgar philosophy, pronounced impossible, and certainly it is a thing of difficulty, and requireth deep search into nature; but seeing there appear some manifest instances of it, the opinion of impossibility is to be rejected, and the means thereof to be found out.

By mid-Miocene, single-needled piñon pines had crossed what is now the Mohave Desert and taken up residence in southern California. After the Miocene came the Pliocene, an epoch of momentous change, when a great uplift raised the towering wall of the Sierra Nevada, shutting off the interior of western North America from the windborne moisture of the Pacific. As the Sierra grew, the interior dried up. Great forests of redwood perished in ancient Nevada as dripping undergrowth gave way to blowing dust.

But the redwood's doom signaled *monophylla*'s opportunity. Aridification of the Great Basin—that sink without a drain stretching from the Sierra to the Rockies—opened up an enormous area to drought-resistant plants. The Madro-Teritiary Geoflora rolled like a carpet across the Basin and north to the Columbia Plateau. Monophyllous piñon pines and junipers, their constant companions, formed woodlands throughout the region. A fossil cone shows that *monophylla* reached the Snake River Valley of Idaho during the Pliocene, and a piece of fossilized wood indicates that a piñon pine once inhabited the San Francisco Bay area.

After the Pliocene came the Pleistocene, when the northern part of the continent was scoured by advancing and retreating ice sheets. Glacial advances chilled the Great Basin, forcing the piñon-juniper woodland southward and off the mountains into low basins and canyons. Subsequent glacial retreats caused warming trends, reversing the woodland migrations.

Today *monophylla* reaches as far north as southern Idaho and northern Utah, where it is found on warm south-facing mountain slopes and outcrops of decomposed granite, sites where competition from other plants is at a minimum. The cooler north slopes are overgrown with a dense growth of faster-growing trees like Douglas-fir, which effectively excludes *monophylla*. However, at the southern edge of its range in Baja California, *mono-*

phylla occurs *only* on the north slopes. In this harsh area
the south-facing slopes are too hot and dry for pines,
while the moister north slopes harbor no serious competi-
tors. Outlying stands at the extremes of the distribution
area are small and widely scattered.

On the east, *monophylla* stretches to the foot of the
Wasatch Mountains and the Utah Plateaus. Small populations are sprinkled throughout Utah's Bear River Range,
minor corridors reach into the Colorado River drainage,
and a long finger points across mid-Arizona into New
Mexico. To the west, it grows in the Sierra Nevada foothills and Tehachapi Mountains, forming a crescent
around the south end of California's Central Valley. From
mountains near Santa Barbara, *monophylla* almost comes
in sight of blue water. Now occupying the middle slopes
of mountains scattered across a vast geographic range, the
piñon pine has probably spread as far as it can under our
present climatic regime.

But an astonishingly varied range it is. Singleleaf piñon
grows with barrel cacti and other Sonoran Desert plants
at 3,200 feet in Paso San Matías, Baja California, and with
bristlecone pine at 9,700 feet on Utah's Frisco Peak. Its
associates include such diverse plants as crucifixion thorn
and white fir; agave and quaking aspen; ocotillo and water
birch. Its ubiquitous companions, however, are Utah juniper and big sagebrush, found with it throughout the Great
Basin.

Edulis also has a broad range of tolerance to environmental conditions. Its northward advance has been halted
by the cold, treeless, sage-covered deserts of Wyoming. In
the south a few populations appear south of the Mogollon
Rim, but these are mainly restricted to cool north slopes,
as in Thompson Canyon in the Big Hatchet Mountains of
southwestern New Mexico. In the west it meets *monophylla* along the margin of the Great Basin, while in the
east a few outlying populations eke out a living on the
high windy plains of the Oklahoma panhandle.

Edulis grows as low as 4,000 feet in Arizona's Oak Creek Canyon and as high as 9,000 feet in the eastern approaches to Monarch Pass in the Colorado Rockies, where it rubs shoulders with lodgepole pine and quaking aspen. Like *monophylla,* it is commonly found with Utah juniper and sagebrush. It also grows with one-seed and alligator junipers, several scrub oak species, and plants of the desert scrub formation. At the forest margin it is often found with ponderosa pine, Douglas-fir, white fir, and Gambel oak.

The diversity of their habitats and associates bears witness to a remarkable store of genetic variability among the northern piñon pines. Such variability is the raw material for continuing evolution, for it buffers a population against future environmental changes that could cause the extinction of a less flexible line.

During the recent past, *monophylla* and *edulis* have increased the genetic variability of their populations even further. Where their ranges overlap, the two species have begun to hybridize, sharing again some of the genes that each had accumulated during a long separation.

CHAPTER 4

Closing the Circle

How Hybrid Trees are Formed

For millions of years the separation of *monophylla* from *edulis* must have been nearly complete. The single-needled species spread across the high ground bordering the western dry-summer deserts, while the twin-needled species secured its hold on the Plateau and southern Rockies. Each adapted to different environments as it went its separate way. But then, probably in the relatively recent Pleistocene past, they again came together.

The repeated migrations back and forth, synchronic with the ebb and flow of the ice sheet, permitted the woodlands to expand into new areas, eventually putting the two species into intimate contact again. Populations of the long-separated species became intermingled along a wide front, curving in an arc from northern Utah, south to Arizona, and southeast into New Mexico. Despite their long isolation from each other, the piñons had not lost the ability to interbreed. Hybrid trees were soon being produced, as they continue to be produced today in the same areas.

Hybrids result when pollen grains of one species fertilize egg cells in the ovules of the other. Pine pollen grains, microscopic pellets of gold dust, are shed in enormous numbers: according to a recent study, a single lodgepole pine shoot produces almost 9 million grains, and it has been estimated that an acre of pine trees produces 5 billion pollen grains. Because of their small size and light weight, pine pollen grains are well adapted for dissemination by wind. In Southeastern pine areas, occasional "sulfur showers" can cover rooftops, cars, and the surfaces of lakes and ponds with a film of pollen. Clouds of conifer pollen can often be seen drifting up canyons in mountainous country, shaken loose by wind in the treetops. In years of exceptionally heavy pollen production, pollen clouds have even been mistaken for the smoke of forest fires.

The distances that can be travelled by airborne pollen are almost legendary. Spruce pollen has been trapped in Greenland, six hundred miles from the Labrador forests where it originated, and the pollen of western shrubs has rained on northern Minnesota after a journey of at least a thousand miles. In species with such mobile pollen, hybridization is possible even without actual intermingling of distribution areas, but hybrids are much more likely to occur where the species share a common territory.

Hybridization between closely related species is fairly common among pines. In northern Alberta, the western lodgepole pine and the eastern jack pine are intermingled, or "sympatric," and freely hybridize with each other. Knobcone and Monterey pines intercross on California's Monterey Peninsula, as do longleaf and loblolly pines in the Southeast. Many other examples can be cited among spruces and other conifers, as well as among broadleaved trees.

Pine hybrids are usually fertile and can breed with each other or with trees of either parent species. Some geneticists believe that hybrids are of evolutionary importance not because of their own qualities, but because they provide a "bridge" for the transfer of genes from one species to another. This process, called "introgressive hybridization," allows the gene pools of both species to be shared and makes possible the flow of adaptive genes from one species to another.

Hybrid pine trees are intermediate to their parents in appearance. For example, hybrids of the northern piñon species (*edulis* X *monophylla*) can be identified in the field by the generous admixture of one- and two-needle fascicles on the same branchlets. Hybrid trees also have fewer resin ducts in their leaves than the *monophylla* parent, but more than the *edulis* parent. Cones of hybrid trees are intermediate in size between those of the pure species.

The tendency of hybrid piñon pines to breed with the parent species ("back-crossing") as well as with each other results in variable populations called "hybrid swarms." In these populations, trees can be found that show characteristics of both parents to a confusing degree. Statistical methods must be used to untangle the complex mixtures of traits.

When pines hybridize, there are no "maternal effects." In other words, crosses of *monophylla* males (pollen donors) with *edulis* females (ovule donors) are no different from crosses of *monophylla* females with *edulis* males.

Natural hybridization of *edulis* and *monophylla* can be observed in three major geographical areas. The most extensive is along the eastern margin of the Great Basin, from Eureka to Cedar City, Utah. The hybrid zone is not always sharply delineated; salients extend westward into the Confusion Mountains of western Utah and the area around Pioche, Nevada. This is *monophylla* country, but apparently *edulis* once grew this far west and left behind a hybrid legacy when it retreated.

A second area of hybridization is in the canyon system of the Colorado River and its tributaries, amid the most spectacular red-rock country of the American West. Hybridized stands are found in at least four national parks —Zion, Grand Canyon, Capitol Reef, and Canyonlands. This is usually considered *edulis* country, but in Zion and Grand Canyons, *monophylla* trees can still be found at low elevations, where they are constant sources of renewal for the local hybrid swarms.

The third zone is the belt of scattered piñon pine groves south of the irregular line of the Mogollon Rim. The mountain ranges dissected out of the Central Arizona Uplift—the Mazatzal, Gila, Apache, Pinal, Bradshaw, and Sierra Ancha—seem to have become Pleistocene refuges for *monophylla* when it was forced northward by the warming trend that followed the last ice age. In these mountains and others, *monophylla* encountered the outliers of the vast *edulis* stands of the Colorado Plateau and, as elsewhere, hybridization occurred.

Barring drastic changes in our climate, these piñon species can be expected to occupy approximately the same areas in the future. Hybrids will probably continue to form along the adjacent edges of their ranges, but it is most unlikely that the hybrids will replace either parent species over large areas. This is due to the evolutionary history of the two species and to the adaptation to its own environment that each has achieved. The hybrids are not "specialized" enough to compete with their parent species in either one's environment and will probably thrive only in the narrow meeting-zones of their parent species.

CHAPTER 5

Rats, Pines, and Pre-History

How Pack Rats Help Man Read the Past

*N*eotoma, the wood rat, a rodent celebrated in western folklore for its arbitrary acquisitiveness, is today helping scientists decipher the past. Several species of wood rat, or pack rat as it is often called, inhabit the western deserts, foothills, and mountains. The desert wood rat, Stephen's wood rat, the white-throated, the Mexican, and the bushy-tailed wood rats are all plentiful in the woodlands of piñon country and in the bordering scrublands and mountains. They are found in the depths of Death Valley and in the cool forests of high peaks.

Desert wood rats like to build their conspicuous cone-shaped houses around the bases of desert shrubs or large cacti, or in crevices between rocks. They haul in dry sticks, the cut stems of plants, fallen leaves, and any other materials that come their way. Bottle tops, tin cans, animal droppings, cones, bones, and stones—all find their way into the house. The nest is a sheltered area deep in the house, lined with shredded piñon bark, or better still, the soft fibers of juniper bark.

White-throated wood rats build houses as high as four feet, with several entrances that lead to the nest. Bushytails conceal their houses amid rocks. Like the other wood rats, they accumulate many bushels of pine cones, juniper berries, sticks, leaves, and pine needles, as well as anything man abandons that is small enough to pick up and is not nailed down. Such houses can be quite numerous, since the wood rats build about three times as many houses as they can occupy at a given time. The ecologist Victor E. Shelford tells of a July night in 1936 when a group of eighteen students saw twenty-one wood rats by lantern light in half an hour. The next day they found sixty-one dens in the area.

Wood rats reserve certain parts of their houses for defecating and urinating. Over the years these "middens" become compacted by constant trampling and encrusted with the residue left behind after the evaporation of endless streams of urine. Gradually, the assortment of plant and animal debris brought into the midden becomes welded together in an indurated mass covered with a shiny surface. Although the wood rat has a very small home range—it usually forages no more than a hundred yards from its den—it drags home whatever it can find in that limited area. Thus, the midden becomes an accidental archive of the flora and fauna of its neighborhood; the wood rat, the unwitting curator of its own herbarium and zoological museum.

Many wood-rat middens are short-lived. The rain washes them out, they are crushed under falling trees or rocks, or they eventually become buried by sediments. But some are constructed in rockshelters or caves, where they are protected from weather and erosion. These can be preserved in the dry desert air for many thousands of years, in the same way that mummies of the "Ancient Ones" are preserved with their artifacts in Southwestern

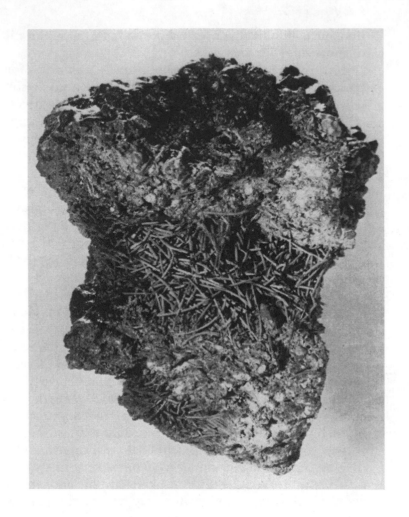

Fossilized singleleaf piñon needles and other debris from a Pleistocene packrat midden found in Arizona. (Photo by T. R. Van Devender)

cliff dwellings. Such middens, replete with plant and animal fragments collected in past ages, are rich sources of macrofossil material.

Since middens are stationary, their contents always represent the local biota. And since plant and animal fragments can usually be identified by specialists with some certainty, the only missing element in the exploitation of a fossil midden for scientific purposes was knowledge of its age. The advent of carbon dating has filled that gap.

Professor P. V. Wells of the University of Kansas, whose field work was in the Mojave and Chihuahuan deserts, was the first to grasp the potential importance of fossil wood-rat middens for studies of the Pleistocene vegetation in North America. The method was also put to intensive use in the Sonoran and Chihuahuan deserts by Dr. Thomas R. Van Devender and his associates in the Laboratory of Paleoenvironmental Studies at the University of Arizona. The first step is to locate middens in well-sheltered locations, an arduous task requiring extensive field work in rough and rocky country. Most of these turn out to be modern deposits containing only plants that still grow in the immediate area. The rare fossil middens can only be identified by finding "extralocals"—the remains of plants or animals no longer present nearby.

Vulture Cave is a typical rockshelter housing ancient midden deposits. Dr. Arthur Phillips III and Jim Mead have found a dozen ancient middens in this tortuous little limestone cave. The entrance to Vulture Cave is an inconspicuous cleft in a fractured rock face barely large enough for a medium-sized adult to wriggle through. It lies just below the rim of the Grand Wash Cliffs, about a thousand feet above the Colorado River in the lower Grand Canyon. It can be reached only by a rigorous climb up steep boulder-strewn slopes studded with spiny cacti and agaves, and guarded by frequent rattlesnakes.

The cave is a claustrophobia-inducing hole, too low to stand in, too dark to see anything without a flashlight, and pungent with the odor of wood rat dung. In addition to numerous plant remains, it has also yielded the tooth of an extinct camel, the jawbone of an extinct ground sloth, and bones of a California condor that last spread its wings here 14,000 years ago.

Midden deposits from rockshelters like Vulture Cave are divided into strata, pried loose, and brought to the laboratory. Here they are subdivided for examination by specialists. The thousands of plant and animal fragments are identified by comparing them to modern specimens of known identity. The resulting lists comprise a flora and fauna of the rockshelter area at some time or times in the distant past.

The final and crucial step is the dating of the fossil remains. This is done in a highly specialized laboratory by the radiocarbon method. Samples of the contents are burned under carefully controlled laboratory conditions, causing carbon dioxide gas to be given off. The gas is then monitored to determine the ratio of the radioactive isotope of carbon (C^{14}) to non-radioactive carbon (C^{12}). These data are used to compute the approximate age of the organic materials.

Van Devender has laboriously catalogued the contents of almost fifty fossil middens he recovered from the Sonoran Desert. Today the vegetation of this area includes such plants as creosote-bush, ocotillo, saguaro, paloverde, and cat-claw acacia. But these are not the species that were collected by the wood rats of the area long ago.

Instead, Van Devender's fossil middens contained plant parts from piñon-juniper and chapparal woodlands. Foliage and seeds of singleleaf piñon and Utah juniper were there in great quantity, as well as one-seed juniper, skunkbush, shrub live oak, Joshua-tree, and algerita; cliff-rose, manzanita, *Ephedra,* and big sagebrush; beavertail, silver-dollar, and staghorn cholla cacti.

These are not plants of the hot and low Sonoran Desert: they require cooler and moister conditions than the desert can provide. One must therefore conclude that this harsh dry area was once wetter and cooler than it is today. In the New Water Mountains near Yuma, Arizona, there used to be a piñon-juniper woodland as low as 1,800 feet above sea level, according to evidence amassed by ancient wood rats. But today one would have to go at least fifty miles to the north and then climb to at least 4,000 feet to sit in the shade of a piñon. According to Van Devender's findings these ancient woodlands have migrated upslope an average of 1,200 feet.

How long ago did the woodland and chaparral plants and animals thrive in what is now one of North America's harshest deserts? Carbon-dating has shown that the fossil rat middens of the New Water Mountains and neighboring Artillery and Kofa Mountains were of late Pleistocene and Holocene age, ranging from 7,800 to over 30,000 years old. During much of that period, the ice sheet lay many hundreds of miles to the north, but its presence affected the climate of the entire continent. Van Devender estimates the Sonoran Desert area to have been 3 to 7 degrees (Fahrenheit) cooler than it is today, with 3 to 9 inches more of rainfall.

Great Basin middens examined by Wells tell a different story. During the late Pleistocene the mountains were in many places covered with forests of five-needled pines: the same limber and bristlecone pines found today at higher elevations. A cool climate prevailed over the entire Basin, leaving no low valleys for the warmth-loving piñon to escape to. As a result, *monophylla* was forced out of the Basin and into the warmer Mohave Desert to the south. Only in relatively recent times, since about 8,000 years ago, has *monophylla* returned to the Great Basin.

In west Texas other piñons were affected by the Ice Ages. About twenty to thirty thousand years ago both Colorado piñon and Texas piñon grew in the mountains near what is now El Paso. Colorado piñon populations extended mainly northwards from here, as they do today, while the Texas piñon continued to the south in numerous ranges east of the Rio Grande and around the Big Bend. Since the last major glacial period Colorado piñon has migrated upslope in its search for a cool ecological zone above what is now desert. But the Texas piñon, unable to tolerate the changed climate, was completely eliminated from its former area along the Rio Grande. Today it is found well east of its earlier haunts, in the Glass Mountains and across the Pecos River on the Edwards Plateau, areas where the winters are milder and rainier than along the Rio Grande.

Much remains to be learned of Southwestern plant communities and paleoenvironments, but thanks to the wood rat's penchant for museum-keeping, a good start has been made.

CHAPTER 6

A Place to Live, Something to Eat

A Tree is What You Make It

Had John Donne been a naturalist he might have said that no organism is an island—and coined the word ecology. Certainly, no pine tree is an island. Piñon pines are participants in a complicated web of relationships with other members of the woodland ecosystem. They are what ecologists call primary producers: that is to say, they use solar energy to convert air, water, and minerals directly into plant substance. By virtue of this ability they provide both food and shelter for more dependent creatures.

For example, their seeds are eaten by woodland inhabitants. One of these is the piñon mouse, a rodent restricted to rocky areas where piñon pines grow and a good enough climber to rustle its own food in the treetops. The big bushy-eared Abert's squirrel, though a heavy consumer of ponderosa pine seeds, often comes down into the woodlands where the pine nuts are much larger. After cutting the cones from their branches, the squirrel strips away the cone scales to remove the nuts and then, in Indian fashion, buries them in underground caches as a hedge against the winter. In *Mammals of Grand Canyon*, Donald F. Hoffmeister tells of an Abert's squirrel that drove away two ravens attracted to its supply of pine nuts. The cliff chipmunk, conspicuous in the woodland for its barking and compulsive tail twitching, not only digs up the nut caches of the squirrels but forages its own pine nuts as well. Other nut fanciers include the rock squirrel, the Uinta chipmunk, and, of course, the wood rats. Perhaps the largest nut-eating quadrupeds are the black bear and the desert bighorn.

Several birds feed heavily on pine nuts, but some of these enjoy a very special relationship to the piñon and will appear in our story later.

Pine nuts are not the only food served up by the piñon. Its phloem—the soft fibrous tissue just inside the dead bark and just outside the wood—is also high in nutritive value. This is the conductive tissue in which soluble sugars and other substances are transported from the place of their manufacture to the place in the tree where they are needed. The major consumers of piñon phloem are rodents—especially the porcupine—and the larvae of bark beetles.

The porcupine is a skilled nocturnal tree climber that gnaws away large irregular patches of the bark of coniferous trees, not only in the Southwest but throughout the western mountain country and across the northern part of the continent. It is equally at home in a Douglas-fir in Montana, a hundred feet up a Sierran white fir, or in a white pine plantation in the Adirondacks. If the porcupine's feeding scar completely encircles a branch or trunk, that part of the tree above the girdle soon dies. Otherwise, the surface of the exposed wood is quickly covered by pitch, and the edges of the wound soon become rimmed with scar tissue, or "callus."

The other major phloem feeders—bark beetle and engraver beetle larvae—are conceived and born inside the tree. Adult males and females of the mountain pine beetle (*Dendroctonus ponderosae*) chew their way through the bark of the piñon, desperately resisting engulfment by the oozing pitch released by severed resin canals. Once inside, they excavate an egg gallery in the phloem and mate, the female spacing her eggs along the gallery. When the grublike larvae hatch, they eat their way around the trunk through the succulent phloem, often girdling the tree and causing its death. There is some disagreement whether the tree dies because girdling kills the roots or because the sapwood is clogged by blue-stain fungi brought in by the beetles. A tree so killed or weakened becomes host to additional "secondary" insects, like woodborers, whose large-bore tunnels may weaken a tree structurally, allowing it to snap off in the wind.

Piñon trunks and limbs can also be attacked by parasitic plants that utilize either the food produced by the tree or the water it pulls out of the soil. Dwarf mistletoes, green flowering plants that do their own photosynthesizing, thrust their rootlike sinkers into sapwood, tapping the tree's supply of water and mineral nutrients and diverting a disproportionate share of its carbohydrate into the grotesque witches' brooms of infected limbs.

The piñon dwarf mistletoe (*Arceuthobium divaricatum*) is found only on piñon pines. Clumps of its sickly, olive-colored shoots protrude from the bark of swollen infected limbs. The dwarf mistletoe plants are leafless and waxy and brittle to the touch. In the fall, their seeds are literally exploded from the fleshy capsular fruits at velocities up to sixty miles per hour, sometimes flying as far as fifty feet. If the sticky seeds land in piñon foliage, they may succeed in infecting another tree. The piñon dwarf mistletoe is probably the single most serious pest of the piñon pines.

Another parasite that attacks piñon stems is the virulent fungus *Cronartium occidentale,* causal agent of the piñon blister rust disease. The fungus is close kin to that causing white pine blister rust further north among the white pines of American conifer forests. But unlike the killer of commercial white pine stands, it is a native of our flora, not an introduced pest. Spores of the fungus colonize leaves of gooseberry or currant bushes alternately with needles of piñon. Thus, the pine infects the currant and the currant infects the pine. The invading fungus grows down through the stricken needle into the twig, then, staying beneath the bark, into a major limb or the trunk itself. Here it attacks the phloem tissue, eventually girdling and killing the tree, leaving swollen trunks with bleeding pitch as evidence of its depredation.

Where pitch oozes from wounds, pitch midges, somehow able to navigate in the sticky flow, feed on the exposed tissues, making their living by adding insult to injury. But others use pitch more constructively. *Dianthidium,* for example, a small black and yellow bee, builds its hive of pine pitch. Where pines are absent, *Dianthidium* is also absent. The small nest of pitch studded with tiny pebbles is inconspicuous in the woodland, tucked into bark fissures or on the underside of rocks.

Pitch may serve still other creatures as a defensive weapon. It has been learned recently that in at least one species of pine, leaf oleoresin is sequestered in the gut of sawfly larvae that feed on the foliage. Since the sticky aromatic fluid can be squirted with considerable force and effect at ants and other predaceous insects, the sawfly benefits doubly by feeding on the needles.

The piñons have some resident sawflies of their own. One of them, called *Neodiprion edulicolus,* is the only insect pest known to have infested large acreages of piñons with serious effect. In 1965 a hundred thousand acres of singleleaf piñons in southeastern Nevada were heavily defoliated. Great numbers of trees were damaged, and many were killed.

Not all sawflies eat foliage, however, and not all are destructive. The members of one fascinating genus of sawflies, *Xyela,* are born in the pollen cones of pines and pass their lives subsisting on the pollen of various plants. The tiny *Xyela* sawflies, about an eighth of an inch in length, are conceived on the surface of pine pollen cones where male and female adults consort. The eggs are placed by the ovipositing female in an incision she makes in the pollen cone just as it is beginning to grow in the spring. The egg hatches and becomes a minute larva that burrows downward through the tissue of the pollen cone until it reaches the base. There it feeds on the yellow dust that is still maturing within the pollen sacs. When, in a couple of weeks, the pollen sacs split open and discharge their pollen clouds into the wind, the *Xyela* larvae drop to the ground and burrow into the soil, where they will pupate.

Different pines are host to different species of *Xyela,* but singleleaf piñon supports two species of this unobtrusive sawfly. Proper timing is the essence of their lives because they live exclusively on pollen, a transient material. *Xyela* adults feed on the pollen of oaks, maples, willows, chokecherry, and other angiosperm trees—whatever is available. But for successful breeding to take place, pollen must be available when the eggs are ready to be placed. Luckily for *Xyela,* the immature piñon pollen cones are emerging from their scales at this very time.

Many other insects are at least partly dependent on piñon pine foliage, but surely the most exquisite relationship between needles and insects involves the needle gall midge. Gall midges are small, soft-bodied flies that have evolved jointly with the trees in which they live. They are found in several pine species including red pine in the Northeast, slash pine in the South, and ponderosa pine in the far West. Professor J. Wayne Brewer and Mark W. Houseweart of Colorado State University have investigated life histories of several gall-forming midges, including the piñon spindle gall midge, fittingly named *Pinyonia edulicola.*

Adult females are orange in color and have two wings. In June, when the shoots of piñon pine are developing from the bud, they lay their tiny orange eggs on the surface of young needles. In about a week the eggs hatch, producing orange larvae which crawl into the crotch between the two needles of the *edulis* fascicle. The larvae commence feeding on the soft green tissue along the inner surface of the needle base. The disturbance caused by the feeding larvae, probably in combination with some biochemical growth substance released by them, stimulates cell growth in the leaf tissue, leading to formation of the gall. Superficially, the gall is a spindle-shaped swelling at the base of the paired needles, but if the needles are spread apart, the halves of the gall are seen to contain hollowed cavities with the feeding larvae inside. These cavities, or cells, become home to the larvae, as many as fifty larvae overwintering in each one. The gall apparently provides the larvae not only with shelter from the elements, but with nutritious food as well. For Brewer has recently shown that the tissue of the gall has a much higher concentration of sugars and starches than is found in normal needle tissue. The next spring, the larvae briefly become pupae and then metamorphose into adults. Mating adults swarm in the sunshine around the piñon pines, and the cycle is closed. The midge's house-building activity kills the galled needles, but this seldom causes severe damage to healthy wild trees.

Just as the midge may be regarded as a parasite of the pine, it is in turn parasitized by a tiny wasp, *Platygaster.* Using her antennae, the female wasp searches out the eggs of *Pinyonia* on the needle surface, penetrates them with her ovipositor, and places her own eggs within them. As the midge egg develops into a larva and then a pupa, the wasp grows within, the shadow of death. Finally, the wasp emerges by chewing its way through the dead husk of its host.

This cycle is a familiar pattern in two-needled pines, and in pines with fascicles of three needles. Several gall midge species inhabit *edulis* and the Mexican piñon, each species forming galls of characteristic shape. But what is especially interesting about the gall midges—at least to the student of evolution—is how they have adapted to single-needle pines, which have no needle crotches to shelter the larvae: how they responded to the challenge posed by the Miocene creation of *monophylla.*

Recently, two new kinds of needle gall midge have been discovered on singleleaf piñon, which had heretofore not been known to harbor any such insects. Each has a unique way of coping with the problems presented by the single needle.

One species of midge makes use of the fascicle sheath scales at the base of the needle. Each *monophylla* needle has about a dozen membranous scales forming the fascicle sheath. Normally, in piñon pines, the dried-up sheath scales become shredded during the first year of a needle's life, and the torn strips roll back like miniature scrolls at the base of the fascicle. In the second year, they usually break off. But the midge fashions these sheath scales into galls. Sheath-scale galls are formed when midge larvae feed between the young sheath scales. In response to the attack, the scales develop into pairs of opposing clam-shell-like shelters for the growing larvae, sometimes four or five pairs forming a circle around the base of the needle. These form excellent cells for the developing midges.

The second gall midge has solved the single-needle problem with one of those subtle checking moves that punctuate the evolutionary chess game. Recall that only one needle forms on *monophylla* fascicles because one of its two potential needle-producing sites is suppressed by

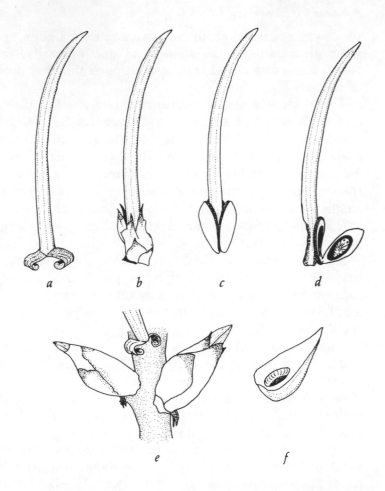

Two types of needle galls have recently been discovered on singleleaf piñon trees in Utah's Grouse Creek Mountains. The sheath scales at the base of a normal *monophylla* needle (*a*) split and curl back, but those attacked by the "needle-scale gall" midge become modified (*b*). The inner sheath scales form four or five clamshell-like shelters (*c*) around the base of the needle, and each of these shelters contains a midge, shown here in the pupal stage (*d*). The midge responsible for the "two needle gall" causes paired needles, instead of singles, to form in each fascicle (*e*). The needles develop as dwarfed fleshy structures, and a midge is sheltered in a cell at the base of each one (*f*). (Drawings by the author)

the monophylly mutation. Our gall midge neutralizes the mutation. The feeding of the larvae *suppresses* the needle-suppression mechanism, allowing both of the potential needles to develop, though they reach only a fraction of their full length. The needles are galled and the larvae grow up in the same type of needle-crotch home as those midges that live in *edulis* and other two-needle pines. Fascicles on the same tree that have not been colonized by the midges produce only the expected single needle.

This type of gall has been found in living pine stands in the Grouse Creek Mountains of northwestern Utah and in central Arizona. Recently, an identical gall with an intact pupa appeared in a fossil rat midden from Burro Canyon, Arizona. With the help of radiocarbon dating, we now know that midges were manipulating the singleleaf piñon over 14,000 years ago, just as they continue to do today.

Animals further up the evolutionary scale also depend on the piñon pine for food. Piñon foliage is eaten, for instance, by the mule deer though it does not seem to be greatly favored. Large herds of mule deer leave the high country to winter in the relatively milder woodlands. An analysis of sixty stomachs from deer of the Kaibab Plateau herd in 1929–31 showed that plants of the woodland made up their entire diet between November and March. In addition to piñon needles the deer also fed on juniper, sagebrush, cliffrose, saltbush, rabbitbrush, and a number of other plants. Piñon foliage is by no means the principal constituent of the mule deer diet, but localized heavy feeding in winter yarding areas sometimes causes the formation of a "browse line": the absence of foliage beneath the height a feeding deer can reach. (Cattle have been known to emulate the mule deer to their own detriment. Pine needles can cause cows to abort their young, a problem of some magnitude to western ranchers. Though most pine-needle abortions have been attributed to the foliage of ponderosa pine, it is suspected that piñon is also unfriendly to cows grazing the woodlands.)

As pointed out early in this book, the piñon nut is a seed without a wing. Thus, unlike the seed of most conifers, it cannot be carried on the wind. Indirectly, though, it does fly, depending on the wings of birds to carry it about. It is now time to examine the complex relationship between piñon pines and piñon birds.

CHAPTER 7

Feathered Cultivators

Birds That Plant Trees in the Desert

To the Shoshone it was known as Too-kottsi. Early American ornithologists called it Maximilian's jay, after its discoverer of 1841, the Prince of Wied. Generations of Westerners knew it as the blue crow, but today it goes by the name piñon jay *(Gymnorhinus cyanocephalus)*. By whatever name, it is not easily overlooked in the woodlands it calls home. It is a large crowlike jay, dull blue in color, with a short tail, a slender bill, a raucous voice, and gregarious habits. Unlike most jays, it is highly social; compact flocks of scores or even hundreds of restless birds may be seen making rapid rolling maneuvers within a hundred feet of the woodland canopy.

The clinical details of the piñon jay's life history are prosaic and straightforward. Pairs nest from late February to April in nests built in piñon, juniper, or ponderosa pine trees. Four to five eggs are usually laid. The nesting females incubate the eggs while their mates form a male flock that feeds together, periodically bringing food to the females. Both parents feed the newly hatched, naked, slate-colored nestlings. In a couple of weeks the young assume a grayish color, including the bill, legs, and feet. After leaving the nest, they remain drably gray until the fall molt, when for the first time they assume a bluish hue. In a year or two, after breeding for the first time, they finally take on the full blue plumage of an adult bird. The piñon jay eats many kinds of insects, berries, and seeds, including piñon nuts. But the way it uses the latter is extraordinary and has helped to shape the evolutionary history of the pine that sustains it.

Late in summer—about the end of August—the seeds of the piñon become ripe. At this time, the cones are still green and pitchy and tightly closed, but the seeds within have well-developed tissues and are of high nutritive value. They are ready to be used. By now, the nesting season is over and nestlings have learned to feed independently. Yearlings have completed their postnuptial molt and, resplendent in their new blue plumage, have fully regained their ability to fly. Thus, the flock is ready for action.

This readiness manifests itself in drama as the flocks wheel and sweep through the woodlands, harvesting the fruit of the pine. Cones are pecked loose from their branches and carried to secure perches where the birds noisily hammer them open and pick them apart scale by scale. The seeds are removed intact, up to twenty being stored temporarily in the jay's elastic esophagus. These seeds are then carried off to the flock's traditional nesting area, as much as six miles away, where they are placed in the ground. Typically, the jay thrusts several seeds into the litter of dead needles and twigs that makes up the woodland floor. Some are deposited on the south sides of piñon trees, where deep snow will not accumulate and where snowmelt will come early in the spring. The cach-

Corvid birds known to eat and to cache seeds of piñon pines. Clockwise from top: Clark's nutcracker, piñon jay, scrub jay, and Steller's jay. (Sketch by Claudet Kennedy)

ing of nuts continues through the fall, and as the cones dry and open, the jays are able to continue the harvest by picking seeds from intact cones still attached to the tree. Their choice of seeds is neither random nor indiscriminate. Piñon seeds usually come in two colors: light tan and deep chocolate brown. Tan seeds in an overwhelming majority of cases turn out to be empty: they consist of a shell containing only the dried-up remnants of an aborted embryo, the common result of an ovule pollinated by a pollen grain from the same tree. In contrast, nearly all of the dark seeds are filled, and most of the filled ones have sound embryos embedded in plump white endosperm tissue.

Piñon jays know all about this: they are piñon seed experts of long standing. They ignore tan seeds, not even bothering to remove them from the cone. Instead they concentrate their harvesting efforts on dark-coated seeds. Here they do not rely on visual cues alone: the piñon harvest is serious business and cannot be left to chance. The foraging jay will remove a dark seed from the cone and "weigh" it in his bill. If it is one of the rare dark-coated empty seeds, it will be discarded. But even if its weight measures up, it may still undergo another test— it may be "clicked" in the bill by a rapid opening and closing movement of the mandibles. Presumably, it must make the right sound, or it too will be discarded. "Bill clicking" appears to tell the jay whether a filled seed contains a normal endosperm, or a diseased or resinous one. Thus, the piñon jay relies on its senses of sight, touch, and sound to reject seeds that would be useless as food.

The fall ends with the woodland litter concealing thousands of piñon seed caches in the areas where the jays will breed next spring. Soon courtship begins, and courting males, chased and beseeched by *kaw*-ing females, feed unearthed nuts to their soon-to-be mates. After egg laying, the incubating females subsist largely on uncovered pine nuts; after the hatch, the young nestlings are also fed

An open singleleaf piñon cone showing the large wingless seeds held in place by membranous portions of cone-scale tissue. Note difference in pigmentation between sound seeds (dark) and empty ones (light). (Photo by Bill Bigg)

the produce of the piñon. Thus is the reproductive cycle of the piñon jay entrained by the rhythm of the wood-land.

The relationship of the piñon jay and the piñon pine is not one-sided; it is clearly a symbiotic one that benefits both parties. The piñon tree accommodates the jay in several ways. It not only produces very large seeds of high nutritive value; it spreads the cone-opening period over several months, making those seeds available throughout the fall. Thus, the bird receives a high-fat, high-protein food in large quantities that can be stored for use at a time when few other foods are available. The concentration of piñon trees in nearly pure stands allows the jay to accumulate a large volume of food in the woodland area near where it will breed. The lack of a seed wing, of course, helps keep the seed in its place on the upper surface of each cone scale until harvested. In addition, a thin membrane of cone-scale tissue (spermoderm) acts as a small "blanket," preventing the seed from falling out of the cone by mere act of gravity. And the tree further obliges by opening its scales widely to expose the seeds to view and by coloring its empty seeds tan, thus advertising to the jay that no effort need be expended on them. The advantages that come the tree's way are equally important. Because they are wingless, piñon seeds cannot be carried on the breeze to the areas of bare soil they need for proper germination and seedling establishment. But seeds harvested by piñon jays are carefully placed in prepared seedbeds, where some will elude the jays' efforts at recovery. These overlooked seeds have a high probability of surviving and becoming trees.

The connection between the piñon jay and the piñon pine is more than a bit of curious natural history. It is, in fact, basic to the ecology of both bird and tree and has provided the dynamic for the evolution of all the piñon pine species.

First, some ecology. Piñon seeds are big and clumsy things, incapable of graceful flight on the wind. If left to its own devices, a tree would eventually drop its seed to the ground beneath its own crown. This does sometimes happen in nature, when the seed crop is so large that not even the jays and rodents can empty all the cones in the fall. In recent years, there have been bumper seed crops in parts of New Mexico (1976), Nevada (1977), and California (1978) that have been beyond the capacity of animals to consume. In the springs following those crops, piñon seeds have fairly littered the woodland floor. In April 1978, I observed thousands of *monophylla* seeds lying on the ground shortly after snowmelt in central Nevada. Hundreds of them were germinating, their stout radicles piercing the pointed end of the seed and turning downward to root in the soil. But with little success. Already, the afternoon sun was raising temperatures to lethal levels, literally cooking the tender radicles before they could go to ground. Seeds germinating in the openings between trees were the first to die; those in the partial shade of sagebrush or tree fared somewhat better, until stray sunflecks and warm breezes heated and dried them out. Clearly, falling seeds would be of little help in the perpetuation of these woodlands.

In order to germinate successfully under conditions that rapidly become arid, the seed must be buried in the moistened soil. How the seed gets there is of no concern to the tree; but that it gets there is clear necessity. This is where the piñon jay, and other members of the "seed-caching guild" come in. By burying seeds for future use as food and by neglecting to remove all of them by spring, the jays set the stage for seeds to germinate.

Of course, setting the stage does not guarantee that the play will be a critical success, for hazards still lie ahead. Rodents have highly developed olfactory abilities and can sniff out the seeds buried in the soil. Seed predation by mice and voles is an important factor in the failure of regeneration in other temperate forests and probably in the piñon-juniper woodland as well. Large rodent populations may make the survival of pine seeds to the germination stage unlikely, unless a year of high seed production and soil moisture availability coincides with one of low rodent populations. Since some rodents cache seeds much as the piñon jay does, rodents are themselves probably responsible for the regeneration of a few piñon trees. Little is known, however, of their effectiveness, and it seems doubtful that these chance germinations could by themselves perpetuate the woodland. On the other hand, there is little question that the systematic efforts of the piñon jay and of the other seed-caching corvids (members of the crow family) are sufficient for woodland regeneration.

While the piñon jay is the chief harvester and cacher of *edulis* and *monophylla* seeds, other members of the crow family also contribute to piñon regeneration. Steller's jay and the scrub jay harvest and cache piñon seeds of one species or another, and Clark's nutcracker comes down from its high mountain home for the seeds of *edulis* and *monophylla*.

Research by Stephen B. Vander Wall and Russell P. Balda in northern Arizona has recently clarified the behavior of the nutcracker in *edulis* woodland. They found that the nutcracker, like the piñon jay, discriminates good seeds from bad and concentrates on trees with a higher than average cone crop. Unlike jays, nutcrackers have a special pouch beneath the tongue for seed transport and can carry as many as ninety-five pine nuts per trip to caching areas as far as thirteen miles away. Vander Wall and Balda's flock of a hundred and fifty nutcrackers stored approximately a ton of seeds in the soil during a single fall harvesting season, and they lived off this stored food well into the spring. It was estimated that the seed caches contained between two and three times the food energy needed to successfully winter the nutcracker flock. This excess suggests that many seeds were left in the ground, free to germinate.

Clearly, the piñon tree and the woodland corvids have a mutual dependence. Tree feeds bird and bird plants tree. Of course, nothing in nature goes smoothly all the time, and the bird-pine relationship is no exception. For example, when the piñon seed crop fails to materialize, the piñon jay must alter its breeding behavior. In the fall of 1968, the piñon crop near Magdalena, New Mexico, was a total failure, and resident jays there were unable to cache a nut supply for the 1969 breeding season. So in-stead of breeding at the usual time, the jays delayed their nuptials until late summer when they could raid the maturing 1969 crop.

Fortunately for them, the 1969 crop was a good one, but even contingency plans don't always work. In 1970 there was another bust: no piñon crop. Therefore, the jays didn't breed in spring 1971. Worse yet, the oncoming 1971 crop was also a failure, which put even late breeding out of the question. Flocks of jays roved nervously that year, unable to breed at all. Fortunately, the spring of 1972 was a wet one, and there were lots of cicadas to eat. This allowed a little spring breeding, but not much. And a poor 1972 piñon crop made even late summer breeding unsuccessful.

Experiments by J. David Ligon at the University of New Mexico suggest a still more intimate twist in the bird-pine relationship. He has concluded that the availability of green piñon cones actually stimulates testis development in male piñon jays at the right time for late summer breed-ing, through some visually triggered physiological re-sponse. Apparently, those brilliant emerald seed cones with their sparkling beads of resin are an aphrodisiac for the garrulous blue crow of the woodlands, persuading him that while late breeding may be poor breeding, it is better than no breeding at all.

If the ecological relationship between the piñons and their feathered cultivators appears close, so is their evolu-tionary relationship. While little can be said as yet about the evolution of the corvids that depend on pine nuts, more can be speculated about the piñons.

The species making up the piñon group are soft pines. They share some unusual morphological features—among others, large wingless seeds and cone scales with the spermoderm modified to hold the seed in place. Therefore, they probably stem from a common ancestral piñon that derived from a conventional winged-seeded

soft pine. For reasons explained in chapter 2, all this probably happened in Mexico. But how did it happen?
The jays provide us our clues. During their own evolutionary history, it became advantageous for jays to cache
food for later use. The widespread use of conifer seeds by
jays of many species suggests that such seeds have been
cached for a long time. As we have seen, seeds cached in
the soil have a good chance of germinating and becoming
the trees of the next generation. If those seeds were picked
indiscriminately from the ancestral soft pines, without
regard to tree, cone, or individual seed character, the act
of caching would have had no evolutionary impact on the
early pines. But if the jays had been selective—if for
example they had preferentially planted seeds from trees
showing certain characteristics—then the jays would
have acted as agents of natural selection, changing the
genetic nature of the pine over the generations.

Take seed size as an example. Most pine seeds are very
small. It may take a very large number of them to satisfy
a jay's caloric needs for, say, a two- or three-month period. A jay capable of discerning differences in pine-seed
size, and intelligent enough to harvest and cache large
seeds first, will be more likely to survive and feed its
young than will a jay with duller perceptions. In the long
run, selection will take place in both pines and jays. Pref-
erential caching of the larger seeds will lead to disproportionate germination of seedlings that, when they mature,
will themselves produce large seeds. And greater survival
of perceptive jays will lead to a more competent jay population that assiduously seeks out large seeds in preference
to small ones.

Several conditions must be met for such a system to
work. For one thing, there must be a good deal of genetic
variation in the pines, so that the jays can have the opportunity of selecting one alternative (large seeds) over another (small seeds). Environmental conditions must also
make it advantageous to the pines to have fewer larger

seeds buried in the soil rather than more numerous smaller seeds scattered over the soil surface. A semiarid habitat fits that description well. Finally, it must be more advantageous to the jays to meet the challenges of that environment by storing food than to move into an ecosystem where storage is not necessary.

This is a greatly oversimplified example, but it illustrates how natural selection can operate simultaneously on jay and pine, modifying both species in the course of time. It seems likely that jays, by selective action over the millennia, crafted a form of tree adapted to growth in semiarid conditions, whose large nutritious seeds attract the very birds needed to plant those seeds and perpetuate the trees' existence. In short, piñons were invented by jays. The jays still hold the patent—and continue to collect most of the royalties.

CHAPTER 8

Man Meets Tree, Tree Meets Man
Beginning A Lasting Relationship

At some unknown time in the past, man discovered the piñon tree. It is impossible to say when, or exactly where in the vastness of Piñon Country, this meeting took place. Perhaps the discoverers were among those early peoples believed to have trekked southward along the western edge of the Great Plains and west into Colorado and New Mexico some 13,000 years or more ago. Such people left few traces, but some evidence of piñon use has been left by ancient inhabitants of the deserts and mountains.

Piñon charcoal and seed coats have been found in the firepits of Gatecliff Shelter in central Nevada. The oldest of these remains have been carbon dated at about 6,000 years of age. Needle fragments indicate that the species utilized was the singleleaf piñon still found around the Great Basin archeological site.

Gatecliff Shelter in central Nevada contains singleleaf piñon remains carbon-dated at 6,000 years of age, and is still surrounded by singleleaf piñon-Utah juniper woodland. The entrance to the rockshelter appears in the lower center of the photograph. (Photo courtesy of David Hurst Thomas, American Museum of Natural History)

Piñon seed coats have also been found with man-made artifiacts at Hogup Cave in northwestern Utah, in strata over 3,000 years old. In eastern Utah, many ruins dating back to the Fremont culture show evidence of piñon use. The people who dwelt in the canyons and on the mesas of this area between the tenth and thirteenth centuries A.D. were corn planters, but archeological evidence shows that they established temporary camps in the woodland and collected and ate pine nuts. Later uses of the piñon pine varied according to the cultural needs of the inhabitants. The Indians of the quintessential Southwest—the high mesas and southern Rockies, what Frank Waters has called the physical and metaphysical center of gravity of the continent—developed agricultural societies of considerable sophistication, and their relationship to *edulis* was a rich and complex one.

For many of the Indians of the Southwest, the piñon was bound up with their very origins. According to the Navaho myth, the piñon was planted by the squirrel, and its nuts, *nictc'ii pináa'*, were believed to have been the basic food of the early people. Similar stories were current on the Rio Grande. The Tewa of the Santa Clara pueblo believed piñon to be the oldest of all trees and provider of *fo*, the oldest food of the people of past days. The pine-nut eaters of long ago used to go up on the mesa to the west. It was there that they gathered and ate fallen piñon nuts, and it was because of these journeys that the people "first knew north and west and south and east." The story is reminiscent of the tradition among the Tewa of San Juan pueblo, as among the Zuñi, that their ancestors came from the northwest; it also correlates with the theory held by some anthropologists that the Pueblo peoples of the Rio Grande Valley are descendants of the Anasazi, the "Ancient Ones" who dwelt in cliff shelters on the Colorado Plateau.

An Indian household found many uses for a pine on the desert's edge. Firewood, for example. Before the white man came, shrubs probably provided much of the fuel used in fires, but the steel axe made it possible to acquire large stores of piñon and juniper. Ethnologist Alfred Whiting felt that the steel axe was indirectly responsible for denuding the Hopi mesas and pushing back the woodland further and further from the ancient villages. The

The cliff dwellings of Mesa Verde, built in Colorado piñon woodland. (Photo by the author)

60   The Piñon Pine: A Natural and Cultural History

same may be true of Monument Valley, where the red sand, eroded out of striking rock formations, blows in the wind, held only lightly by the sparse cover of desert shrubs. The picturesque Navaho shepherd is partially— perhaps overwhelmingly—responsible for the barren earth his people dwell on, but the steel axe may share in this responsibility. For two hundred years or more, Monument Valley has been in the process of desertification. At one time it must have been at least a marginal woodland, for today there are still scattered junipers on the slopes. Occasional piñons even cling among the inaccessible rocks, out of the reach of axes and the deadly mouths of sheep and goats.

Juniper wood burns evenly with a quiet flame lacking dramatic effect: it was, therefore, preferred for the cooking fire. Piñon firewood comes into its own on dark nights in midwinter, when warmth and cheer and a bit of excitement is needed. Nobody who has sat before a roaring, pitch-boiling, bubbling, scented fire of piñon can think of it as the mere consumption of wood. It is the spirited release of centuries of brilliant sunlight absorbed under a cloudless Southwestern sky, the sudden and instant flow of energy patiently accumulated.

The piñon was much used in construction of many sorts. Sometimes a whole tree became a Navaho shade house for summer occupation. When this was done, the lower limbs were cut off and their stubs sealed with mud. It was not without reason that the Zuñi called this tree *he'sho tsi'tonně,* the "gum branch"; any unsealed branch stubs dripped sticky pitch on the unwary visitor. The Navaho also made extensive use of *cá'ol,* the piñon, as a source of hogan poles, roof beams, and such carved items as tool handles, looms, and saddletrees.

The gum oleoresin or pitch of the piñon tree had many important uses in piñon country. The Navaho boiled it with sheep's and goat's hooves to make glue, which they used to cement turquoise into silver settings. The Hopi also used it as a cement in turquoise mosaics. When mixed with a decoction of sumac leaves and yellow earth, pitch was made into a black inklike dye for coloring wool and blankets. But one of the most important uses of all was in waterproofing basketry water jugs. Melted gum was poured inside the jar, which was then turned until the entire inner surface was coated.

Pueblo and Navaho Indians used piñon gum to give their stone griddles a nonsticking surface, like an early Teflon. Ruth Underhill has described how a Pueblo woman prepared the griddle on which she will make the wafer bread of blue cornmeal.

> Under the chimney hood is the nearest approach to a stove that the Pueblos had. This is an oblong stone, mounted on two long low ridges of clay, so that a little tunnel is formed under it. In this tunnel the fire is placed where it is protected from drafts and can heat the oven like a griddle.
>
> It sounds simple but the stone which can serve such a purpose must have been through a long preparation. It must be smooth sandstone to begin with, then its surface must be soaked with oil, generally from sunflower or squash seeds, though buffalo fat is good if you can get it. Our hostess and her sisters used squash seeds which they chewed and spit out on the stone, after it had been gradually heated. It was a ticklish business for if the temperature were changed suddenly, the stone would crack.
> . . . It took them almost a day to get the stone properly heated, rub the squash oil into it and then rub it again with wads of piñon gum, which melted and sank into the pores. They finished by scrubbing the stone with juniper and pine twigs, which left it clean and slightly scented.

Other household uses for pitch by the Hopi included the repair of broken pots and the varnishing of wooden throwing sticks.

The piñon was a mainstay of native medical practice in the Southwest. The Navaho and Hopi routinely used pitch for dressing open wounds, alone or mixed with tallow and red clay. This practice was widely emulated by white settlers and survives even today in rural areas of the Southwest. The fumes of burning gum were inhaled to cure head colds and earaches, and buds were chewed up and spit on burns. Inner bark, sometimes eaten during hard times, was also a wound dressing; needle decoctions were drunk to relieve symptoms of coughs, headache, colds, flu, and fever.

Matilda Coxe Stevenson, who made many visits to the great pueblo of the Zuñi from 1879 to the early 1900s, tells how syphilis was treated there:

> The needles of the (piñon) tree were given for syphilis. The patient chews the needles, and after swallowing them drinks a quantity of cold water and then runs for about a mile, or until he perspires profusely, when he returns home and wraps in a heavy blanket . . . Frequently, a tea is made of the twigs and drunk warm in conjunction with the needles. The ulcers are scraped with the fingernail until they bleed, when the powdered piñon gum is sprinkled over them. If there is swelling at the groin, it is lanced by the attendant theurgist and the powdered gum sprinkled into the incision as an antiseptic.

But perhaps the most powerful piñon medicine was that used among the Zuñi, by the members of the Sword Swallowers order of the Great Fire Fraternity. After a ceremony they ate the young shoots of ponderosa pine if they wanted their wives to bear sons; but if they wanted daughters, they ate the tender shoots of the useful, domestic, reliable piñon.

Piñon figured in ritual practice, healing, and ceremonialism literally from the cradle to the grave. When an infant Apache girl outgrew her cradleboard, her mother would place it in the crown of a young piñon pine, on the east side, and she would tell the tree, "Here is the baby-carrier. I put this on you, young and still growing. I want my child to grow up as you do." Among the Navaho, the cradleboard of a dead child was placed in the crown of a piñon, as were the worn cradle laces of healthy, growing children.

The piñon was a place to put other things too. On the ninth day of *Keldzi Hatal,* the Night Chant, the Slayer of Alien Gods and The Child of the Water placed their corn-husk cigarettes in the shade of a piñon. After the cere-monial of the male branch of Shootingway, ritual things were placed on a young piñon tree at sunrise, and the patient cautioned not to visit ancient ruins, not to injure a young piñon tree, and not to stand over another person. The female arrow in the male branch of Shootingway was of lightning-struck mountain mahogany, fletched with down from the underside of an eagle wing and wrapped with buffalo sinew and charred piñon gum.

On the fourth day of the Night Chant, when performed for a male patient, the Talking God carried in his hand a piñon sapling stripped of its branches. The incense of the Night Chant was provided by the burning of piñon gum. The ceremonial wands and pokers were of piñon wood, selected from branches that grew on the east, north, west, or south sides of the tree.

The pollen of piñon pine, removed in the spring from the numerous small pollen cones borne in the lower parts of the crown, was much in demand as a ceremonial item among the Navaho. Night Chant medicine included pol-len of piñon, juniper, and ponderosa pine; in the Wind Chant ritual these pollens were combined with ground-up prairie clover and wild buckwheat, mixed in water, and drunk by the patient. A similar tonic was taken dur-ing the Mountain Chant, with the addition of wild par-snip and ground berries of chokecherry and sumac. Piñon pine wood was valued even after it was consumed by fire: Navaho medicine men pulverized the charcoal, which they considered the best blackening for the sand paintings used in healing ceremonies.

Boughs of piñon and juniper were used in building antelope corrals. These funnel-shaped enclosures, up to two acres in area and with walls twelve feet high, were used to trap the driven animals in the Corral Way ritual of the Navaho. A ring of branches formed the circle for the Mountain Chant, in which the Navaho dancers carried bunches of piñon foliage. And on the last night of the Mountain Chant, a stuffed weasel was seen sticking his head above a basketful of Douglas-fir and piñon branchlets.

Piñon went to sadder ceremonies, too. Before burying the dead, the Navaho smeared pitch on the body, and the mourners placed some under their own eyes and on their foreheads. Among the Hopi, after the deceased was laid to rest, the survivors went back to his house and put piñon gum into the fire, purifying their bodies and their clothes in the pungent cleansing smoke. Piñon gum had preventative powers, too. Among the Hopi, a dab on the forehead before going out of doors in December gave protection against sorcerers.

CHAPTER 9

Food That Grows on Trees

Prospering in the Great Nut Grove

Despite its many other uses, physical and metaphysical, the piñon pine's greatest service to the native American was as supplier of food in a harsh land. When the hand-to-mouth hunters of the north discovered the nut-pine groves, they discovered the Southwest and became the custodians of the vastest orchard on Earth's surface. Although no grove, no tree, would produce heavy crops every year, it was almost always possible to find some canyon, some mesa or sierra, where nuts were locally abundant. By caching surplus nuts, a prudent household could lay in a hoard that would last the winter.

One can speculate how the availability of pine nuts on the great Colorado Plateau made it possible for the early Anasazi cliff dwellers, the "Ancient Ones" or Basketmakers, to adopt the cultivation of maize. Initially, they lived for many centuries as hunters of game and gatherers of natural produce. But as they developed networks of communication with other tribes, they learned of the corn-plant cultivated further south. Eventually, they themselves took up the growing of corn—there is ample archeological evidence to prove it—but there must have been generations of experiment, of trial and error, while they adapted the new crop to their dusty mesa tops. Learning how and when to deep plant, to build check dams, to weed; how to select strains fitted to the new environment; how to grind the kernels, enhance their nutritive value by alkali processing, and incorporate the new food into their diets: this knowledge took time to accumulate. Meanwhile, the availability of a relatively reliable wild crop lent Anasazi life a modicum of stability, allowing refinements to be made in the new agricultural technology. The great piñon groves within which many Anasazi villages were located surely provided the basic nourishment of the people, as Navaho and Pueblo tradition still holds. It has been estimated that about 85 percent of the archaeological sites in Utah are in piñon-juniper woodland, as are many other Southwestern ruins, including those of Mesa Verde.

Among Indians of historic times, the collection of piñon nuts was a family affair. The Indians of the pueblos, like the Tewa of Santa Clara and the people of Jemez and Cochiti, set up temporary camps in the mountains when seedfall began. They would spend several days picking seeds off the ground and shaking the trees to catch the seeds in outspread blankets. The completed harvest was then packed in wagons and taken home. When they arrived home, the nuts were roasted on the griddle and put away in jars until winter. Elsie Clews Parsons has captured the spirit of this event:

> Presently Matia goes into the storeroom, the third room
> of this three-roomed house, for his saddle and bridle; he
> has a day of *piñon* gathering ahead of him and he plans
> to ride to the mesas to the east. This is a good *piñon* year,

such as occurs every seventh year, says Matia, and people gather enough of the crop to last them three or four years. The other day the whole household went, in their wagon; but today only Matia sets forth, on horseback. . . . After sundown on my return to the house I find Matia back. He looks tired, and he says he is. But there in the corner of the inner room stand two bulging bags. *"Muncho piñon,"* says Juanita with great satisfaction, *"muncho piñon."*

To the Pueblos the nut pines were not private property, and pickers were free to seek their crops wherever the pines grew, even at the edge of a neighboring village.

The Navaho also camped in the nut groves for the harvest, sometimes remaining until snowfall. Some Navahos used oak poles to beat the cones from the trees, but others feared the spirit of the Bear would make them ill in retaliation; the usual practice was to pick seeds from the ground. Of course, a wood rat's cache was greatly valued, and the innovative Navaho later used wire-mesh screens to sift the woodland litter.

Different methods were used by the tribes of *monophylla* country. They lived in the Great Basin or near the Mohave Desert, dry-summer deserts not as well stocked with game and food plants as the summer-rain country of the Navaho and Pueblo peoples. For them, the piñon harvest was a more serious business. They could not afford to wait until the cones opened, when they would have to compete with birds and rodents.

They went into the mountains late in August or very early September when the cones were still green and tightly closed. These "early" cones could be stored for the winter, or opened by fireheat for immediate use. A hooked stick was used to beat the cones down, or to pull branches down for easy picking, preferably on cool mornings when the pitch was less sticky on the cones. The Gosiute band of Shoshones called the stick *aihkon;* to the Hualapai it was *digatúa.* The Gosiute of Utah and Nevada, the Hualapai of northwest Arizona, the Panamint of

Woodland of Colorado piñon on the slopes of Escudilla Mountain, Apache National Forest, Arizona. The tall tree on the left is a ponderosa pine. (Photo by U.S. Forest Service, Southwestern Region)

Death Valley, and the Cahuilla of the San Jacinto Mountains packed their green cones to camp, threw them on piles of dry brushwood, and set the piles afire. The swift flashy fire served to open the cones, so that the seeds would come loose from the cavities of the cone scales, called *he-push,* or cone "eyes," by the Panamints. At the same time the nuts were roasted. John Muir has left us a vivid description of the *monophylla* nut harvest, as it was undertaken by the Mono Lake Paiute about 1870:

When the crop is ripe, the Indians make ready the long beating-poles; bags, baskets, mats, and sacks are collected; the women out at service among the settlers, washing or drudging, assemble at the family huts, the men leave their ranch work; old and young, all are mounted on ponies and start in great glee to the nut-lands, forming curiously picturesque cavalcades; flaming scarfs and calico skirts stream loosely over the knotty ponies, two squaws usually astride of each, with baby midgets bandaged in baskets slung on their backs or balanced on the saddle-bow; while nut-baskets and water jars project from each side, and the long beating-poles make angles in every direction. Arriving at some well-known central point where grass and water are found, the squaws with baskets, the men with poles ascend the ridges to the laden trees, followed by the children. Then the beating begins right merrily, the burrs fly in every direction, rolling down the slopes, lodging here and there against rocks and sage-bushes, cached and gathered by the women and children with fine natural gladness. Smoke-columns speedily mark the joyful scene of their labors as the roasting fires are kindled, and, at night, assembled in gay circles garrulous as jays, they begin the first nut feast of the season.

The readiness with which Indians would drop their work-for-wages and head for the hills at nut time caused anxiety among the white settlers of Nevada's Snake Valley in 1875. Mr. Levi Gheen was the interpreter at a tense council meeting between settlers and Gosiutes at the home of Mr. Lehman, where the following exchange took place:

Question: Why did all the Indians flee to the mountains
at about the same time?
Answer: For the past four years there have been no pine
nuts in this country. This year there is a great plenty
and as has been the custom in former years when the
pine nuts were ripe, word was sent out to all the Indians
to gather in parties in the mountains and have their
dance and Pine-Nut Feast.

Thus were the fears of the settlers put at ease, and rumors of gathering war parties spiked.

Nuts were stored in *ollas* (earthenware jars), baskets, or hide bags. The Navaho secreted quantities of nuts in pits two to six feet below the surface, in the groves where they picked them. The Northern Paiutes stored nuts in grass-lined pits called *hū kí va,* and green cones in stone-lined bins from which pine nuts could be extracted as needed.

The nuts were basically a winter food. To some, like the Great Basin Shoshone, Northern Paiute, and Washo, they were the stuff of life itself, the staple food without which winter was a time of disaster. To the Pueblos, *piñones* were a snack, enjoyed and prized, but no longer the necessity they had been in antiquity when they were "the old food of the people"; now the people were affluent and lived in great houses above their river-bottom cornfields.

The Chumash of the southern California coast relished pine nuts, but they lived at the very edge of piñon country, and like many other of the early Californians their staple was the oak acorn, available in huge quantities and supplemented with fish and seafood.

Pine nuts were eaten in various ways—raw, roasted, or boiled; whole or ground into a flour on the *metate.* The Navaho mashed their oil-rich *edulis* kernels to a rich tasty butter *('atlhic),* like peanut butter, which was spread on hot corncakes. The Northern Paiutes ate whole *monophylla* nuts boiled in water, or they mashed them and prepared

A basket of singleleaf piñon nuts about to be winnowed to separate out needles and other debris. (Photo by Margaret Wheat, from *Survival Arts of the Primitive Paiutes,* University of Nevada Press)

a soup or mush to be sucked from the fingers. This could be eaten hot or cold—or even frozen, according to a Paiute informant who compares frozen mush to "popsicles" and prefers to eat it with strips of rabbit meat.

The Northern Paiutes prepared nuts for eating by roasting them twice. Freshly extracted nuts were first shuffled about in a shallow basket with live coals. They were then shelled on a *metate* by the rubbing action of a hulling

The shells of these freshly roasted singleleaf piñon nuts are being cracked by the gentle crushing motion of a hulling stone. (Photo by Margaret Wheat, from *Survival Arts of the Primitive Paiutes,* University of Nevada Press)

stone. After the shells were winnowed away, the kernels were roasted a second time.

Pine nuts were one of the few foods permitted a Paiute mother for the twenty-two days immediately after childbirth. In her classic book on Paiute survival arts, Margaret Wheat tells of a woman whose grandmother warned her always to stir her pine-nut soup with a stick. "Her grandmother knew a woman who 'used her hands, and pretty soon she died.' "

CHAPTER 10

Reading Nature's Message

Early white travelers in the Great Basin spoke with contempt of the seminomadic Indians who dwelt there, collectively terming them "Diggers" and dismissing them as uncivilized and brutish. The appellation stemmed from the Indians' spring and summer food-gathering activity, the digging of edible roots in the valleys and along the snow-fed tributaries. Such gathering is necessarily a low-density occupation and was conducted by small family bands that had little contact with each other during the root-gathering season. They camped in casual temporary brush shelters as they foraged, and they supplemented their warm-weather diet of roots and seeds with occasional catches of fish and game. Only the rare winter traveler, like Major John Charles Frémont, grasped the fact that the really critical food resource in the Basin was the *monophylla* nut crop. But even the perceptive Frémont missed the deeper significance of the nut crop—its central role in the culture of the Washo, Shoshone, and Paiute people of the Basin.

Typical Great Basin woodland of singleleaf piñon and Utah juniper in Nevada. Snake Range in the background. (Photo by the author)

The Great Basin includes most of Nevada, the western half of Utah, and small parts of several neighboring states. It has no drainage to the sea: instead, its waters flow inward, collecting in depressions like the Great Salt Lake, Pyramid Lake, and the Carson and Humboldt Sinks. Much of its flowing water passes directly back into the desert air through evaporation, without first being impounded in a lake or marsh. The lakes and their surrounding marshes and salt flats cover only a fraction of the area of the Great Basin, which consists mainly of alternating valleys and abrupt mountain ranges. The map of Nevada has been likened to an aerial view of an army of caterpillars crawling towards Mexico. The "caterpillars" are the short parallel fault-block mountain ranges, oriented north and south, rising boldly from the intervening desert basins. Because of their elevation they condense moisture from the Pacific air passing over them and receive more rain and snow than the valleys below. Thus, while the valleys support grass amid sagebrush and shadscale, the taller of the mountains harbor coniferous forests on their upper slopes. In the intermediate zone lies the woodland of singleleaf piñon and Utah juniper.

Great Basin winters are not to be taken lightly. Snowstorms follow one another like waves breaking on a beach, packing the high mountains in deep powder. Between these Pacific-bred storms, incursions of arctic air often follow a southward-dipping jetstream deep into Nevada and Utah. Under such conditions, reliance on the hunt becomes impracticable, little better than substituting death by exposure for death by starvation. In winter, much time must be spent indoors, simply enduring. And to endure, one needs to stockpile a staple food in quantities that will last until spring. Meanwhile, one sits securely by the fire telling stories, scraping hides, and mending equipment.

The cultivation of maize brought this kind of security to the people of the Colorado Plateau and the Rio Grande, but the Great Basin peoples were not so fortunate. The difference in lifeway is due largely to a difference in summer climate. In that enormous alkali sink, the frost-free growing season is often short and the summers dust dry. No frequent afternoon showers awaken the seed of the cornplant or rapidly mature it in the heat of summer. No broad rivers with sandy flats are inundated by flash floods in July and August. Instead, the cloudless skies breed dust devils. Thus were the Indians of the Great Basin denied maize. For many years, the early people must have found life in the Basin precarious, even foolhardy. They probably learned slowly what they needed to know about the nut pine and its message of survival. To see how they did this, we must first learn something about cones and seeds.

Like most trees of the temperate zone, piñon pines produce their yearly growth of new branches by extending or stretching out their buds. The buds are formed in the summer and remain dormant under a protective cover of scales until the following spring. They are like miniature branchlets telescoped together before all the parts are fully formed. If a branchlet is going to bear seed cones, these will first become evident as microscopic white domes within the winter buds. Most cone-bearing buds are in the range of half an inch to an inch in length, and they are usually borne on the faster-growing branches of the tree. In spring the buds elongate, and their needles quickly develop, giving the new shoot a spiky look. At this point, the emerging cones—or conelets, as they are often called—are spiny little pincushions ranging in color from pale yellow green to red purple, and about one-fourth of an inch in diameter. Each scale of the conelet bears on its upper surface two tiny ovules that are potential seeds. Shortly after the conelet emerges, it spreads its scales. Wind-borne grains of pollen, produced in pollen cones on other shoots of the tree or on neighboring trees, sift into the ovules; the pollinated conelet then closes its scales, sealing the pollen grains within. The conelet grows slowly during the summer, finally becoming a prickly brownish sphere about half an inch in diameter. In this condition it passes the winter.

The following spring, the yearling cone starts to grow again. The pollen grains inside its ovules become activated after a year's lapse and fertilize the egg cells deep within the ovules, starting the process of seed formation. Throughout the summer the now-green cone enlarges. The seeds mature in late summer, and the cone, now about three inches long, brilliant emerald green, and glistening with pitch, stops growing. In the autumn the cone dries, its scales part, and the mature seeds are displayed in the opened cone.

Thus, it takes three separate growing seasons—and about twenty-six months of elapsed time—to produce mature pine nuts. During this long developmental period there are several stages when the potential seed crop is especially vulnerable. Early in the first spring, when pollen grains are being formed by meiotic divisions in the male cones, a sudden severe cold snap can damage the chromosomes, causing inviable or sterile pollen to be formed. Later in the spring, when conelets are emerging and pollen is ready to fly, climatic conditions can also intervene. A late spring freeze can play havoc with tender young conelets, "frost burning" them wholesale and destroying the potential crop over an entire drainage basin. Heavy and prolonged spring rains can keep the pollen cones from releasing their masses of golden grains, leading to low rates of pollination and the premature dropping of the conelets, which apparently require a hormonal substance provided by the pollen to stay on the tree. In later stages the growing cones can be attacked by beetles and cone moths whose feeding tunnels destroy the infested cones. In years of small crops these depredations can be especially severe, sometimes accounting for most of the crop.

As maturation approaches in the final summer, chipmunks raid the cone-bearing trees, cut down the cones, gnaw them open, and eat the seeds. Other rodents, like the piñon mouse and the wood rat, collect and store seeds found on the ground or picked from open cones. Piñon jays sweep through the woodland like wildfire, eating and caching great quantities of nuts.

In addition to all these external threats to the crop, there is an inherent limitation built into the tree itself. Foresters have long been aware of cycles of good and poor seed years, at intervals of varying length and consistency, but often of the order of three to seven years. A bumper crop in a particular grove is seldom followed by another bumper crop: in all probability it will be followed by one or two lean years. The reason for these ups and downs in seed production is not entirely clear. In part, it may be the result of weather cycles, but we do not yet know enough about the specific effects of climatic factors to be sure. Another possible explanation is that trees simply cannot marshall the necessary carbohydrates needed to construct large numbers of cones and seeds more than once every few years. There is evidence that such a nutritional limitation causes seed cycles in Douglas-fir, but it has not yet been demonstrated in the more complex pines.

With the nut crop so variable both in time and in space, a reliable food supply could only be gathered if the gatherers paid close attention to the maturation of the crop over a period of many months. And pine-nut crops were indeed closely observed. Lalla Scott has described how the Northern Paiutes decided where and when to harvest the piñon crop:

> Every year the Indians take their families to the hills to gather pinenuts, just as they have done for ages. When Pascal was head man in the village, it was he who had to go before the middle of August and scout to find out the conditions of the trees, and see if the nuts were plentiful or scarce and bring back a few cones and call a powwow.

All the Indians of the village come for the ceremony. Men, women, and children dance in a circle. The chief or head man of the village stands in the center of the big circle and offers thanks to the Big Man for the nuts they had last year, and asks in prayer for a better crop this year. Then they begin their dance, again in a circle. The chief gives out the cones to men who test them for quality and ripeness. They know from this test how many days before they should go out to gather the pinenuts. This is almost always the first week of September. The pinenut powwow ceremony usually lasts all night. But if the Paiutes decide that the crop looks poor and there will not be enough pinenuts for the people, they break two or three pinenut cones, put them in water, and dance two or three nights —sometimes even an entire week. The season for picking pinenuts lasts for three weeks or until the first heavy frost.

Usually, there was at least a marginal crop in most areas. The Shoshone are said to have tolerated freedom of harvesting in each other's territories, but this was apparently not the case among the Paiutes of Owens Valley, California. According to the late Julian H. Steward, pinenut territories were owned by "districts," and trespass led to quarreling and rock-throwing incidents. John Muir claimed that white men were actually killed for felling piñon trees but cited no details for corroboration. The Northern Paiutes considered the nut groves as property and even charged money of whites for the privilege of cutting down groves around Dayton, Nevada.

If they were armed with timely intelligence on the whereabouts of a crop, and if the crop was not in a zone prohibited to them, the Indians of any area should have been able to secure their winter food hoard. How such intelligence was acquired and disseminated by the Western Shoshone of the Reese River Valley has been a subject of investigation by anthropologist David Hurst Thomas of the American Museum of Natural History. According to Thomas, in the fall, when piñon harvest time arrived, Shoshone bands would come together at a prearranged site. There they would harvest nuts, conduct communal rabbit drives, and hold an annual festival. The piñon festival was the social highlight of the year and was often attended by several hundred people. At night, after the rabbit drives, there was dancing—the round dance, the horn dance, the back-and-forth dance. There was gambling among the men and courting among the young. Marriages were arranged and sexual liaisons conducted. Trading, the presentation of gifts, and mourning of the dead were all features of the piñon festival.

A similar festival—the "Gumsaba," or Big Time—was observed by the Washo, another people dependent on the pine nut. After four days of ritual and celebration, the Washo would disperse into the woodland for the harvest, establishing winter villages there. Thomas has described these settlements, using as evidence the archaeological remains left behind by the Shoshone:

> The piñon winter villages were located on the ecotone between the sagebrush flats and the piñon-juniper belt. The camps themselves were located on low, flat ridges. Water was generally within a quarter mile, but these villages were rarely situated directly on streams or springs. There are several possible reasons for this, the most obvious being a reluctance to scare the local game animals from water. Additionally, snow was on the ground during these winter months, obviating the necessity for running water. Cold air drainage down mountain canyons also made the ridge tops more attractive. Bark or grass-covered domed huts probably served for shelter . . . In the winter village, the primary subsistence item was the family store of piñon nuts, supplemented by game—probably antelope and mountain sheep.

Thomas thinks that the Western Shoshone arranged their piñon festivals a year in advance so that, at each festival, notice could be given of the following year's assembly area. But to do this, the participants must have been able to predict likely areas of good harvest a year before the crop was mature. With pines such a prediction is indeed possible. Recall that more than two years are required for the nut crop to mature, and the cones are visible for about fifteen months prior to maturation. It would be risky to predict a *good* crop a year in advance because of the still unmeasured depredations of weather, jays, insects, and rodents. But it would be a simple matter to recognize an area where the crop would be *poor,* because there would already be a paucity of developing cones. Such information was brought together at the piñon festival and used in choosing the site of the next festival. No cultivated food crop has the long developmental period of the pine nut, or crop futures that can be told so far in advance.

According to this view, the piñon festival was used as an opportunity for regulating the future size and distribution of Shoshone populations. If at the festival the intelligence from all areas foretold a failure of next year's crop, then measures could be taken to prevent mass starvation. The measures, often draconic, were necessary for the group's survival. Births could be limited by sexual abstinence or abortion. One or more twins could be killed at birth, as could illegitimate children (many of whom were probably conceived at other piñon festivals). The sick and the old could be abandoned. A widow might be killed and buried beside her husband. These were the kinds of decisions that had to be made by desperate people seeking to survive. Again, it was only the long developmental period of the pine-nut crop that permitted the Shoshone to regulate their population to a size commensurate with the future food supply. Just as life on the plains was fitted to the habits of the buffalo, life in the Great Basin was fitted to the homely, thin-shelled nut of the singleleaf piñon. And it was the annual piñon harvest that gave focus to the Great Basin year, that enriched the lives of its people beyond what Jacob Bronowski has called the "life without features" of the common nomad.

CHAPTER 11

The Piñon in Indian Myth

The piñon tree, its edible nuts, and its pitch are commonly encountered in stories told by the Indians of piñon country. Some of these tales, like the first two of the sampler below, explain natural history. Another teaches the necessary housekeeping lesson of how to remove pitch from one's hands. Several embroider the fabric of legend that surrounds such characters as Rabbit, Fox, and Coyote. The final tale explains a great historic event of significance to natives of the Southwest and Mexico.

1. How the Pine-Nut Tree Came to Nevada (Shoshone)

Blue Crow was standing on a tall rock watching the Indians playing football. After a while he started to choke and coughed up blood. He choked because of the north wind that came from pine nuts far away. Blue Crow flew to the north and found the pine-nut trees. He brought pine nuts back with him and planted them all around here in the mountains. Those pine nuts were a lot bigger than the ones we have today. It's a long story and would take three or four nights around the campfire to tell it all.

2. Why Piñon Trees are Dwarfed (Washo)

Many years ago the Wolf-god created a river and taught the Washo people to bathe in it. The people were content and came to gather piñon nuts in the fall. This was when they had Gumsaba, the Big Time; when they feasted, sang, and hunted together.

When Coyote-god saw the people were happy, he became jealous of Wolf-god. He warned the people not to bathe in the river, that it would make them old and he would eat them. The frightened people did as Coyote-god said.

Then a great drought came and dried up the river. Fires burned up the piñon trees. With the trees gone there was no food. The rabbits went away, so there was no fur for blankets. The Washo suffered and many of them died. Finally, Wolf-god came back to help them. He scattered arrowheads across the hills and valleys so that the Washo could hunt wherever they wished. But the jealous Coyote-god poisoned the arrowheads, to kill anyone picking them up.

Wolf-god then scattered pine nuts on the hills and caused them to grow into a new forest like the one that had been destroyed by fire. When he saw the Washo were too weak from hunger to climb up for the pine nuts, he tore off the treetops and dwarfed all the pines. The Washo then went among the dwarfed pine trees, picked the nuts from their low crowns, and became strong. They had Gumsaba again in the fall, and they sang and danced, hunted, and ate pine nuts together.

3. Taking Off Pitch Gloves (Paguate Pueblo)

One day when Fox and Rabbit were in the hills looking for food, they found a piñon tree oozing lots of pitch.

Rabbit started to gather the pitch until he had a big pile of it. "What are you going to do with it?" asked Fox. "I am going to make a pair of gloves for you," said Rabbit. Then Rabbit put pitch all over Fox's hands and took her over to the piñon tree.

"Now hit the tree with your right hand," said Rabbit. Fox hit the tree as hard as she could, and her hand stuck to the tree. "What shall I do now?" asked Fox. "Hit the tree hard with your other hand," laughed Rabbit. Fox's other hand also stuck to the tree. Then Rabbit put gloves on Fox's feet also, and soon all of Fox's hands and feet were stuck to the piñon tree.

Rabbit went away laughing, but after a while he felt sorry for Fox and came back to the tree. He tried to get Fox loose, but the pitch was too sticky and it held Fox fast to the tree. So Rabbit went for help.

Soon Rabbit returned with Wood Rat, who said he could free Fox from the piñon tree. Wood Rat chewed on some animal fat and smeared it on Fox's hands and feet. Soon the pitch loosened, and Fox was free.

4. The Pitch Man in the Cornfield (Laguna Pueblo)

Once there was a man who had a cornfield. He worked in his cornfield every day, but got little out of it, because most of his corn was being eaten by Rabbit.

One day he asked his friend how he could catch the thieving Rabbit. His friend advised him to go into the mountains and find some piñon pitch. "Make a pitch man and put it on the edge of your field, where Rabbit will see it."

The man followed his good friend's advice. He went to the mountains and brought back enough pitch to make a very sticky pitch man. When the sun went down, he put the pitch man in the cornfield where Rabbit would be sure to see it.

When Rabbit came to the cornfield that night, he saw the pitch man blocking his way. "Get out of there," he said, "get out or I'll hit you!" The pitch man would not move. "Move or I'll hit you with my paw," said the belligerent Rabbit. The pitch man still would not move.

Rabbit finally struck the pitch man with his paw, and his paw stuck. He hit with another paw, and it stuck also.

When all his paws were stuck, he bit the pitch man with his teeth and his mouth stuck.

In the morning the man found Rabbit all stuck up with pitch and killed him. Rabbit's wife and little ones saw the pitch man and ran away. They did not go again to that cornfield.

5. How Rabbit Escaped from Coyote (Hopi)

Coyote was angry. He had been hunting rabbits and had finally caught one. But Rabbit had fooled Coyote and escaped.

Rabbit now lay in a burrow deep in the ground where Coyote could not reach him. Each time he stuck his long nose in the burrow, Rabbit would go in a little further. This made Coyote even angrier.

"I will kill you!" said Coyote. He took some flint and steel from a pouch and set fire to a bundle of grass. He blew the smoke into the burrow hoping to kill Rabbit. But Rabbit just laughed at him, "I eat grass, it cannot kill me!"

Then Coyote found pieces of piñon wood, and Rabbit became scared, because rabbits have no use for piñon. Coyote put the bark and the gum into the burrow and set it afire with burning twigs. Rabbit was frightened and when Coyote put his nose into the burrow to blow smoke, Rabbit kicked the hot melting gum into Coyote's face. The gum stuck to Coyote's face. It burned him badly and blinded him long enough for Rabbit to come out of his burrow and escape.

6. Coyote and Badger on Second Mesa (Hopi)

Coyote and Badger had pretended to be people. They had dressed in stolen shirts, moccasins, and eagle feathers and had gone to Oraibi for the kachina dance. They had looked handsome in their stolen clothes and had stayed two nights with some pretty Oraibi girls. Then the girls had married them, and the men of Oraibi became angry with Coyote and Badger.

First the men tried to take the girls back by hunting more rabbits than Coyote and Badger. But Coyote and Badger killed fifty rabbits each, and none of the Oraibi men could kill more than twenty. So Coyote and Badger kept their wives.

Then the men and boys of Oraibi challenged Coyote and Badger to a foot race. They would run from the Pali't-spi spring to the foot of the big mountain. Some of the Oraibi boys ran fast, but they became tired early and Coyote won the race. So Coyote and Badger continued to keep their wives.

Finally, the chief told the people that the only way to get back their girls was to take them by force. Coyote and Badger saw that all Oraibi wanted to kill them, so they took their wives and went back in the night to Coyote's home where their grandmothers lived. Next morning after breakfast, the Oraibi people gathered up their picks and shovels and hoes and went down to Coyote's house which was down in the ground to the west of Oraibi. The people started to dig Coyote and Badger out of their house, so the two friends had to dig faster and go deeper. Soon Coyote's and Badger's grandmothers came out and threw a basket of cedar berries among the people. The hungry people stopped digging and ate the berries. Then the grandmothers threw a basket of piñon nuts among the people, and the people stopped digging again and ate the nuts. Then the grandmothers threw a basket of cooked rabbit meat among the people, and the people put down their tools and ate the meat.

Meanwhile Coyote, Badger, and their wives dug for a long way and came to the surface and escaped. They went to On'ansika, on the other side of the woods.

7. The Birth of Montezuma (San Juan Pueblo)

Many years ago there lived in San Juan a beautiful young girl. All the girls and women of the pueblo hated her because they were jealous of her beauty. She, in turn, hated the other people and had little to do with them. She lived with her grandmother in two small rooms.

One autumn there was a good crop of piñon in the mountains, and many of the villagers were preparing to go up for the harvest. The beautiful girl knew she would not be invited, so she followed the others at a distance.

On the way to the mountains she stopped to rest, and as she sat there, she heard a voice speak to her. The voice told her to go back, and to empty and clean out her two small rooms. "Close the rooms for four days. When you open them on the fourth day you will find one filled with white corn. No matter how much corn you use, the room will always be full, and you will be the Queen of the White Corn." The voice told her that the other room would be full of piñons. When she opened the door, a piñon bigger than all the others would roll out, and she was to swallow it.

The girl went home and told her grandmother what the voice had instructed her to do. She obeyed the command and on the fourth day opened the two rooms. When the villagers saw that the first room always stayed full of corn, they were greatly impressed and named her "Gue-ch-ayuh," the Queen of the White Corn.

When she opened the second room, a big piñon rolled out, and she took it and swallowed it. Nine months after swallowing the big piñon, she gave birth to a baby boy, whom she named Son of the Sun. He was Montezuma.

CHAPTER 12

Better Than Those of Castile
Men on Horseback Come to Piñon Country

The piñon witnessed the coming of the white man everywhere in the Southwest. But more than a passive witness, it was a participant in the success of his arrival. A revisionist view of western American history could easily be based on the role of the piñon in sustaining the early Europeans.

The first Spanish subjects to see *edulis* were also the first Europeans to visit the Southwest: those doughty survivors of the catastrophic expedition led by Panfilo de Narváez. They were Alvar Núñez Cabeza de Vaca, Alonso del Castillo Maldonado, Andrés Dorantes de Carranca, and his slave Estevanico the Black, also known as Black Stephen. From 1528 to 1536, this party wandered westward across the continent from their shipwreck in the Gulf of Mexico, across Texas, New Mexico, and part of Arizona, into Sonora and then south along the coast of the Gulf of California. In his *Naufragios y Comentarios,* Cabeza de Vaca says of some unidentified Indians of southern New Mexico: "They ate prickly-pear fruits and pine nuts; there are in that country small pine trees and their cones are like little eggs, but the nuts are better than those of Castile because they have very thin shells."

Cabeza de Vaca reported that the Indians "grind the nuts with the shells and eat them as meal," and he also told this to Gonzalo Fernández de Oviedo y Valdes who put it all down in the so-called "Joint Report." But he may have been mistaken. Even ground nut shells are abrasive and indigestible, and with all the other problems of survival they had to face, the Indians were no more likely than their Spanish visitors to resort to an unnecessary masochism. Cabeza de Vaca may have been confusing two separate operations involving the use of grinding implements: the first, the cracking and removal of the shells; the second, the grinding of the kernels into a meal or flour.

The route taken by Cabeza de Vaca has been the subject of controversy; some versions have him skirting New Mexico by as much as 200 miles. A scholarly and exhaustive study has been made by Cleve Hallenbeck, who for many reasons, including geographic details of pine distribution, makes a convincing case for a route from west Texas through New Mexico and southeastern Arizona, rather than one extending deeply southwards into Chihuahua and Sonora. Also, Cabeza de Vaca's description makes it clear he was referring to *edulis,* not the thick-shelled Mexican piñon. While *edulis* shells are easily cracked with the teeth, those of Mexican piñon require judicious use of hammer or pliers. This bolsters Hallenbeck's case because a route traversing Chihuahua would encounter the thick-shelled piñon only.

In *Piñon Country,* Haniel Long credits the availability of pine nuts with the very survival of Cabeza de Vaca and his companions. If so, the piñon pine has cast a long shadow, indeed, for when the tattered survivors reached Mexico, their arrival touched off a series of historically important expeditions into New Mexico. The earlier of these, including Estevanico's ill-fated visit to the Zuñis of

Hawikuh (who killed him), were stimulated by fabulous tales of the Seven Cities of Cibola. They led directly to Coronado's bold incursion of 1540 and ultimately to the colonization of New Mexico by Juan de Oñate in 1598.

Coronado's deep thrust into piñon country marked the end of the Southwest's age of innocence. His chronicler, Castañeda, in describing Cibola (Zuñi) and its inhabitants writes that "the country is all wilderness, covered with pine forests. There are great quantities of the pine nuts. The pines are two or three times as high as a man before they send out branches." He described a fine woodland indeed. Castañeda also saw "a sort of oak with sweet acorns, of which they make cakes like sugar plums with dried coriander seeds," and he noted that the Zuñis "collect the pine nuts each year, and store them up in advance." The country between Cibola and Tiguex (on the Rio Grande) was not pleasing to Castañeda, for it was covered with woodland junipers and piñons: "There are not fruits good to eat in the country, except the pine nuts."

Among the famous accomplishments of Coronado's lieutenants were the discoveries of the Grand Canyon and the Hopi mesas. The Canyon was first viewed by a party of soldiers led by Don Garcia Lopez de Cardenas from the south rim, a country "elevated and full of low twisted pines, very cold, and lying open toward the north." Far below lay the "Tison" (Firebrand) River, which "looked from above as if the water was 6 feet across, although the Indians said it was half a league wide. It was impossible to descend."

The discovery of the Hopi mesas—Tusayan to the intruders—was credited to Don Pedro de Tovar, who deceived the inhabitants and subdued them, finally receiving as tribute "some dressed skins and corn meal, and pine nuts and corn and birds of the country. Afterward they presented some turquoises, but not many."

A later expedition was led by Antonio de Espejo, "resident of the city of Mexico, native of the city of Córdoba, [who] made at the close of 1582, in company with fourteen soldiers and a Franciscan friar [a journey] to the provinces and settlements of New Mexico, which I named New Andalusia in remembrance of my homeland." The adventurers passed "through mesquite groves and cactus fields, and over mountains wooded with pine forests producing piñon nuts like those of Castile."

Almost two centuries later, in 1776, while events of moment were underway on the continent's eastern seaboard, heroic travellers were exploring piñon country. One of them, Fray Francisco Garcés, a Franciscan priest of San Xavier del Bac in Arizona, traversed the piñon-clad Tehachapis and other ranges of Mohavean California and reached the nut lands of the Hualapais in Arizona.

Further east, two other Franciscans, Fray Francisco Atanasio Domínguez and Fray Silvestre Vélez de Escalante struck north from Santa Fe in search of a safe route to the California missions. The route actually taken by the expedition, as described in Escalante's journal and a notable map by the retired soldier Captain Bernardo Miera y Pacheco, led into western Colorado, across Utah, and (in abandonment of the original plan) south and east into Arizona and back to Santa Fe via the Hopi country.

On September 4, 1776, during the nut-gathering season, the exploring party encountered three Ute women and a child and accepted from them chokecherries and piñon nuts. Other nut-eating Indians were met along the edge of the Great Basin in Utah, but the friars had little interest in these tribes and repeatedly inquired about other tribes that grew corn. Corn planters were considered more civilized and thus more easily converted to the Faith.

By mid-October, the party was low on food and suffering discomfort from the cold. Miera was too weak to walk. On the nineteenth, Indians who called themselves the Yabuincariris brought the hungry aliens many bags of piñon nuts as well as grass seed and cactus fruits. But even this good luck had its costs, if we can credit Escalante's diagnosis, for a few days later Lorenzo Olivares, having become uncontrollably thirsty from eating too many pine nuts, stayed out of camp all one night in search of water, causing his companions "much worry."

By October 23, the party, sick from grass seed and weak from hunger, bought from Indians "a fanega of piñon nuts," enough to last only a few days. Escalante's journal for October 29, written while camped on the rocks near Lees Ferry on the Colorado River, poignantly expresses the plight of his party:

> Not knowing when we might leave this place, and having consumed all the flesh of the first horse, and the piñon nuts and other things we had purchased, we ordered another horse killed.

But by the grace of their sponsor, and with the help of pine nuts and other provender, Escalante's party finally arrived safely in Santa Fe. Miera's map recorded for future travellers the availability of an important resource, indicating in the *"Provincia de Nabajoo"* a "Land of mesas covered with trees that give a fine pine nut, junipers, and others of various species."

Their familiarity with pine nuts stood the Spaniards in good stead, as shown also by the experience of Juan Cristobal, a boy of ten or twelve, in 1808. Juan's village in New Mexico had been attacked by Apaches and the boy taken captive. For a month he lived as a prisoner, but he was finally able to make his escape early in October. For almost a week he wandered furtively through the woodlands, subsisting on ripe piñons. On October 7, he was found by a column of Spanish soldiers under Captain Francisco Amangual. The soldiers were not a search party. They were exploring a route from San Antonio, Texas, to Santa Fe, and came upon the boy purely by chance.

Woodland of Colorado piñon and Utah juniper in Canyonlands National Park, Utah. (Photo by the author)

Pine nuts have not saved Spaniards only, but Anglos further north as well. The history of the settlement of California might well be very different if not for the nut of the singleleaf piñon, *Pinus monophylla*. Here are the words of John Bidwell, who led the first emigrant wagon train to California in 1840:

> We were now camped on Walker River, at the very eastern base of the Sierra Nevadas, and had only two oxen left. . . . Looking back on the plains we saw something coming. . . . To make a long story short, it was the eight men who had left us nine days before. They had gone further south than we, and had come to a lake, probably Carson Lake, and there had found Indians, who supplied them plentifully with fish and pine nuts. . . . The men had eaten heartily of fish and pine nuts and had got something akin to cholera morbus. We ran out to meet them and shook hands, and put our frying pans on and gave them the best supper we could. Captain Bartleson, who when we started from Missouri was a portly man, was reduced to half his former girth. He said, "Boys, if ever I get back to Missouri I will never leave that country. I would gladly eat out of the troughs with my hogs."

History does not record whether Captain Bartleson ever got his wish, but if he did, he had pine nuts to thank for the opportunity.

A few years later, history repeated itself just a few miles away. Major John Charles Frémont, sometimes a reckless leader, had maneuvered his expedition into the Sierra Nevada in the dead of winter. It was January 24, 1844, and the party was nearly out of food. Frémont's account of what happened that day has about it the flavor of high adventure.

> A man was discovered running toward the camp as we were about to start this morning, who proved to be an Indian of rather advanced age—a sort of forlorn hope, who seemed to have been worked up into the resolution of visiting the strangers who were passing through the

country. He seized the hand of the first man he met as he came up. . . . He brought with him in a little skin bag a few pounds of seeds of a pine tree, which today we saw for the first time. . . . We purchased them all from him.

At this time Frémont's party was in the vicinity of the Walker River, but the exact route they followed has not been satisfactorily established by historians. On the next day a dozen Indians came into camp to trade pine nuts, which Frémont now shrewdly discerned as "the staple of the country." "Whenever we met an Indian, his friendly salutation consisted in offering a few nuts to eat and to trade." The Indians were probably Washo. Frémont noted heaps of empty cones lying on the ground, where the seeds had been gathered the previous fall. On January 29th:

> The Indians brought in during the evening an abundant supply of pine nuts, which we traded from them. When roasted, their pleasant flavor made them an agreeable addition to our now scanty store of provisions, which were reduced to a very low ebb.
> . . . The Indians informed us that in certain seasons they have fish in their waters, which we supposed to be the salmon trout; for the remainder of the year they live upon the pine nuts, which form their great winter subsistence —a portion always being at hand, shut up in the natural storehouse of the cones. At present, they were presented to us as a whole people living upon this simple vegetable.

In the summer of 1846, a force of seventeen hundred American soldiers, regular Dragoons and Missouri volunteer infantry led by Colonel Stephen W. Kearny, marched from Fort Leavenworth, Kansas. Their objective was to take the surrender of New Mexico from Governor Armijo in Santa Fe. Their thousand-mile march was punctuated with hardships as they met the desert and its hazards for the first time. Again, piñon proved a timely resource. The journal of Lt. George Rutledge Simpson of the Missouri Volunteers records his first purchase of pine nuts in the village of San Miguel, between Las Vegas and Santa Fe. He found them "oily and not unpalatable." After the occupation of Santa Fe, goods became scarce and prices high, but one commodity was always available and plentiful. On October 28:

> Corn meal is scarce and is worth $5 a *fanega*, which is about two and a half bushels. The commissary purchases flour at $4.50 per bushel, and mutton at $1.50 a carcass, butchered and dressed. Melons are still abundant in (the) market, and *piñones* in any quantity.

About two years after Major Frémont's introduction to pine nuts came the most dramatic rescue that can be attributed to what he called "this simple vegetable." Winter came early to the Sierra Nevada in 1846. On October 28 of that year, five feet of snow was hindering the climb of a beleaguered group of California-bound emigrants—the Donner-Reed party. Already weak from hunger and plagued by deaths, these pioneers were soon to be halted by the early storms and forced into winter quarters at Donner Lake. The tragic story of this band has often been told, but historians have failed to emphasize that the ultimate rescue of the survivors—more than forty men, women, and children—was by the grace of half a cup of pine nuts.

On December 16, 1846, fifteen of the party, calling themselves the "Forlorn Hope," made a desperate final attempt to cross the Sierra for help from the California settlements. Carrying only six days' supply of food, they blundered through the deep drifts on improvised snowshoes until, on the tenth of January, they came upon an Indian village. Several of them had perished on the way. For a week they rested under the care of the friendly Indians. But even a week's rest and their diet of acorn bread brought scant improvement to men and women half dead of hunger and exposure. The leader of the Forlorn Hope, William H. Eddy, was sickened by acorn bread and unable to keep it down. Years later Eliza P. Donner Houghton told how Eddy gained back his strength on January 17, 1847:

> ... the chief with much difficulty procured for Mr. Eddy, a gill of pine nuts which the latter found so nutritious that the following morning, on resuming travel, he was able to walk without support.

After leaving the village, Eddy alone of the party was able to continue with Indian guides. He covered eighteen miles that day to reach the cabin of Colonel H. D. Richey, and for six of those miles the trail was marked with his blood. A relief party was immediately formed which the next day rescued the six surviving members of the Forlorn Hope. A later relief party penetrated the snows of Donner Lake the following month. The success of the rescue efforts can be attributed to the nutritive value of a handful of pine nuts. The Donner party may have been saved by the nuts of local Digger pines (*Pinus sabiniana*) or of singleleaf piñon traded from the nearby Washo.

Why didn't the hard-pressed emigrants collect piñon nuts along their route through Nevada? During the height of the piñon season they passed Pilot Peak, the Ruby Mountains, Battle Mountain, and the Humboldts. On October 19, they were at Wadsworth, at the foot of the Virginia Range. At any of these places they could have gathered a stock of piñon nuts that would have seen them through the winter, but they did not try. Their journals never mention piñons. Were they ignorant of the value of pine nuts, despite the experiences of earlier travelers? Did their hostility to the Indians they encountered along their route discourage the Indians from offering piñons in trade, as they had done with Bartleson and Frémont? We can only speculate on their failure to live off the bounty of the pine nuts.

And what of today? In this era of ultraprocessed, plastic-wrapped, hydrogenated, homogenized, and synthe-

sized foods, is there a place for wild nuts gathered from
the cones of little desert pines? Can the Indian's staff of
life still save Westerners *in extremis?*

Kelly Warren could say *yes*, with emphasis. Kelly was
a fourteen-year-old deer hunter who got lost on the San
Carlos Indian Reservation in Arizona in the fall of 1974.
For four days he wandered in the woodlands, like Juan
Cristobal a hundred and sixty-six years before. And, like
Juan Cristobal, he lived on the piñon nuts he was able to
shake from cones until he was reunited—not with the
Spanish cavalry—but with his parents, his health still
unimpaired and his ardor for the hunt undiminished.

The hungry traveler who happens to be in the Southwestern woodlands during nut season joins four hundred
years of pioneer company when he tastes the fruit of the
pine. Raw or roasted, it can be a life saver.

CHAPTER 13

Pine Nuts as a Foodstuff

We do not usually think of coniferous trees as suppliers of food, at least most Americans do not. A recent book, intending to tell laymen all they need to know about trees and forests, pronounces that conifers "benefit few other kinds of life, providing no food for man and little for birds and animals."

Father Escalante learned better from Indians who knew better. The Russians, the Swiss, the Australian Aborigines, and the Indians of South America all knew better. In fact, so many peoples have known better that we can only account for our lapse by pleading selective ignorance, the kind of ignorance that can lead a Donner party to starvation. Perhaps we have a bias against "gathered" food, identifying it with savages too primitive to find their food behind a plow or in front of a gun. Savages gather: men farm.

Modern tree books seldom have much to say about food from wild trees, but minds were not always so narrow. See, for example, the 1858 classic by George Gordon, *The Pinetum: being a synopsis of all the coniferous plants at* present known, with descriptions, history, and synonymes, and comprising nearly one hundred new kinds. Gordon mentions no less than ten pines and three *Araucarias* as species of coniferous trees supplying food for man. A full list would be even longer.

Both Colorado and singleleaf piñon are marketed on a small scale in this country from one coast to the other. Mexican piñon is a common item in the back-country marketplaces of Chihuahua, and Nelson piñon is commercial further south. Sierra Juárez piñon used to attract people of the Colorado delta country into the rugged mountains of Baja California, where they came into conflict with Franciscan missionaries. The Tepehuan of Chihuahua eat seeds of the Mexican White Pine *(P. ayaca-huite)* in the western Sierra Madre.

The seeds of two Rocky Mountain pines were once utilized by Indians: limber pine *(P. flexilis)*, which was eaten also by Idaho and Wyoming settlers; and whitebark pine *(P. albicaulis)*, whose tightly closed cone scales guard nuts with unsurpassed delicacy of flavor.

California is rife with nut pines, as John Muir knew, but most recent tree students seem to have forgotten. The towering sugar pine *(P. lambertiana)* of the Sierra Nevada, tallest of the world's pines; the limby Coulter pine *(P. coulteri)* of Southern California; the windswept Torrey pine *(P. torreyana)*; and the spindly Digger pine *(P. sabiniana)* of the foothills—all have yielded their seeds for man's use. In fact, the name "Digger pine" derives from the pejorative term for the Indians who ate its nuts.

Pine nuts are of outstanding dietary value. In Table 1 the large edible nuts of piñons and some other pines may be seen to compare very favorably with pecans, peanuts, and walnuts in protein, fat, and carbohydrate content.

Of the piñons, *cembroides* is richest in protein and lowest in starch, and singleleaf piñon is lowest in protein and starchiest. Colorado piñon tends to be richest in fats and is comparable to Siberian stone pine, which is

Table 1.   Dietary Value of Some Pine Nuts
and Some Commercial Nuts.

Type of Nut	Protein (percent)	Fat (percent)	Carbohydrate (percent)
Colorado piñon, *Pinus edulis*	14	62–71	18
Singleleaf piñon, *P. monophylla*	10	23	54
Mexican piñon, *P. cembroides*	19	60	14
Parry piñon, *P. x quadrifolia*	11	37	44
Digger pine, *P. sabiniana*	30	60	9
Southwestern white pine, *P. strobiformis*	28	52	7
Italian stone pine, *P. pinea*	34	48	7
Siberian stone pine, *P. sibirica*	19	51–75	12
Chilgoza pine, *P. gerardiana*	14	51	23
Pecan, *Carya illinoensis*	10	73	11
Peanut, *Arachis hypogaea*	26	39	24
English walnut, *Juglans regia*	15	68	12

Percentages are approximate and are based on shelled nuts.

pressed commercially for the production of cooking oil. One pound of shelled Colorado piñon nuts provides 2,880 calories, more than the food energy in a pound of chocolate, and nearly as much as in a pound of butter. The biologic value of its protein exceeds that of all commercial nuts but the cashews and is comparable to that of beefsteak.

Just as important as protein content is protein quality. Proteins are made up of amino acids. All twenty of the amino acids are found in the nut protein of both Colorado and singleleaf piñon. The value of Colorado piñon in the diet of Indians of the Southwest may lie partly in the fact that of the nine amino acids essential to human growth, seven are present in greater quantity in piñons than in cornmeal. Eight of the nine essentials are more abundant in *monophylla* than in *Amaranthus,* an important food plant of Great Basin Indians. Both *edulis* and *monophylla* nuts are especially rich in tryptophan and in the essential sulfur-containing amino acid cystine. The fats of the piñons are also of high food quality. The most abundant fatty acids in *edulis* and *monophylla* nuts are the unsaturated oleate, linoleate, and linolenate, which comprise about 85 percent of the total fats. *Edulis* nuts are extremely rich in phosphorus (2,740 milligrams per pound—about the same as soybeans) and in iron (24 milligrams per pound). They also contain significant amounts of vitamin A, thiamine, riboflavin, and niacin.

Clearly, the piñon pine was a food source of great value to early native Americans. While this was an important reason for their reliance on the piñon, it was not the only reason. A subsistence food must more than repay the energy expended in its collection and processing, and *piñones* satisfy that requirement. Fortunately for the people who coveted them, the pine nuts formed concentrated masses of food that could be collected with a high degree of efficiency.

Estimates of how many pine nuts can be collected in a day vary, and it is difficult to gauge their reliability, but they can be taken as educated guesses. Picking the nuts from the ground after seedfall, it is said, can yield a collector twenty pounds a day. Shaking a tree at the right time, and catching the nuts with a blanket, a collector can accumulate perhaps seventy pounds. Up to a hundred and fifty pounds of nuts can be collected daily by a husband and wife raking up the woodland litter immediately after seedfall and separating out the nuts with wire mesh screens. A favorite Navaho trick was to rob a packrat's nest of its accumulated wealth of nuts. A large cache would yield the equivalent of a day's effort, and presumably the rats were expected to replenish their missing booty. According to Walter J. Perry, a government forester of half a century ago in New Mexico, as much as four *almudes* of nuts could be removed from a packrat hoard. An *almud* is a Spanish cubic measure, equivalent to about eleven pounds of piñon nuts.

According to estimates made by the late anthropologist Julian H. Steward, individuals of the Owens Valley Paiutes gathered as much as forty bushels of nuts in a season, a figure also cited by John Muir. A Paiute informant from Fallon, Nevada, reports that in good seed years he provides his family with three gunny sacks (about three hundred pounds) of their favorite winter food. About 30 percent of the seed weight of *monophylla* is made up of shells, while the thicker-shelled *edulis* has a waste factor of about 42 percent.

Piñon nuts have probably been articles of commerce since shortly after the first Indians came to the Southwest. Near Fort Collins, Colorado, in Owl Canyon, an isolated stand of *edulis*, many miles north of its main distribution area, forms the extreme northeastern outlier of the species. The trees grow in an area of broken limestone terrain between the Rocky Mountain front range and the sweeping Great Plains (one might add that they may not grow there much longer because they occur on an outcrop of rock that is being quarried for use as road fill). The oldest trees in the grove are all about four hundred years of age and grow together in a clump. Professor William Weber of the University of Colorado and C. W. Wright, who have studied this plant community, believe it originated from piñon seeds dropped by Indians using an ancient trade route between the northern plains and the piñon country.

The land of the Navaho nestles among vast forests of piñon pine, and Navaho tribesmen often sold or traded their surpluses to the Zuñi, to the Hano pueblo of the Hopi mesas, and to such Rio Grande pueblos as Santa Clara and Jemez. In the early 1800s, the annual caravans plying the *Camino Real* between Santa Fe and Mexico City brought south such valued produce as wool, hides, pine nuts, and the finest El Paso brandy.

Throughout the twentieth century, pine nuts have continued to be an item of commerce. It is practically impossible to measure the true dimensions of this "cottage industry" because neither the U.S. Department of Agriculture nor anyone else compiles regionwide statistics on wild crops. But a few figures have been published over the years, and they give a hint of the commercial standing of piñon nuts, or at least, of *edulis*.

In 1909, nuts sold at retail in the Southwest brought 40 to 60 cents a pound, and 5 to 15 cents of this went to the picker. The 1921 New Mexico crop, which totaled 600 tons, brought only 20 cents a pound, of which 10 cents went to the pickers. In 1936, the New Mexico crop was larger—about 4,000 tons—and most of it went to large Eastern cities, especially New York. Some of that year's Arizona crop came from the Navaho Reservation, where one trader alone paid $18,000 for *piñones*. That represented about 25 cents a pound for the pickers and was a welcome income supplement for poor Reservation residents.

During the period 1915–1939, about 16,000 tons of pine nuts were legally harvested in the national forests of New Mexico. A Bureau of Indian Affairs estimate places the 1960 harvest at about 125 tons.

Fewer data are available for *monophylla* nuts, reflecting, perhaps, a taste preference for the oilier *edulis*—or maybe a lesser tendency of Great Basin Indians to go into the commercial market. William M. Maule has calculated figures for one shipment of nuts made in 1930 from Reno, Nevada. Four carloads of nuts totalling 70 tons were collected by local Indians, for which the pickers earned $35,-000 (25 cents a pound). This was made up of about 135 million nuts gathered from 6 million cones that weighed 375 tons!

The retail price of pine nuts in the West has risen substantially in recent years. In 1976 the State Forester of New Mexico found raw piñon nuts selling for nearly $4.00 a pound in Santa Fe stores, shelled and roasted nuts for $7.60. The price fluctuates somewhat with good and poor crop years. At least one major national food distributor has gone into the pine-nut business, but only in a small way. Meanwhile, nuts of the Italian stone pine are quite widely available in shops specializing in "health foods" and "organic foods," where they are sold under the name "pignolias." These nuts have extremely thick shells, difficult to crack with the teeth, and are usually sold shelled.

The food potential of piñon forests in the Southwest has never been reliably estimated, but it is enormous. There are undoubtedly many wild crops producing great quantities of food appreciated by few people only. The piñon is prominent among them.

CHAPTER 14

Science Finds the Piñon

In the middle decades of the nineteenth century, science came to piñon country. It came in the form of American and European naturalists—botanists, zoologists, mineralogists—who travelled independently or with military columns. The naturalists regarded new plants and animals not only as gifts to mankind but as feathers for the ornamentation of professional caps. To the botanist, a "new" plant is one that has not yet been collected, published in a valid scientific journal following prescribed procedures, and given the legitimacy of a Latin name. With the opening of the Southwest, botanists gained access to the habitats of hitherto undescribed plants, giving them the exciting opportunity to "make" many new species.

The first piñon pine to be recognized by science was *Pinus cembroides,* the Mexican piñon. This species was first collected by Wilhelm Karwinski in the state of Hidalgo, probably in 1831, and was described by the botanist Zuccarini in 1832.

The next piñon presented to the American botanical community, in 1845, was the singleleaf piñon. We have

already seen how Major John Charles Frémont described
his dramatic discovery of this tree, which provided "the
mainstay" of Great Basin existence. Now let us look at
Frémont's preoccupation with his new tree after the con-
clusion of his expedition.

Frémont attached a great deal of importance to his for-
tuitous discovery of the Great Basin piñon. Perhaps he
was struck by its cultural importance, or maybe he was
animated by the desire to get credit for discovering the
species. Whatever the motive, he seems, in retrospect, to
have been almost obsessed with the fate of his new tree.
On December 30, 1844, just three months after his return
to Washington, he wrote the noted botanist John Torrey,
"I enclose you some of the seeds of a species of Coniferae
(No. 367 of 1844) and found more numerously in 1843.
These seeds contribute largely to the support of Indians
& I am anxious to know what the tree is." (Actually, this
is at variance with his official report, which states that he
first saw the species on January 24, 1844, at the lower edge
of snowy mountains.) On January 12, 1845, Frémont
wrote Torrey, then in his prime and recognized as the
nation's leading botanist—what it is almost inconceivable
he would think necessary to tell him—that the seeds
could be found by looking between the scales of the cone!

Having almost satisfied himself that Torrey would now
find the nuts, Frémont proceeded to call the botanist's
attention to the unique single needles of the new species.
On February 26, 1845:

> 367.1844 A remarkable species. Without cones. Probably
> a *Pinus* though the leaves are almost all *solitary!*—only
> two or three being found double in the same sheath.
> Washington City Feby. 26. 1845.

> My Dear Sir:
> In looking over the list of plants the words which I have
> underscored in the above struck me for the first time to-
> day, & I (have) to tell you that in the first box of fossils
> which I sent some weeks ago to Dr. Hall, was a cone for

you in good preservation belonging to that tree. . . . I am
very much interested in this particular tree.

In fairness to Frémont it should be pointed out that
there is no published record of Torrey having answered
his urgent letters. By late March, Frémont's earlier anxi-
eties had apparently been put at ease, but he became
concerned that Torrey would not do a prompt and proper
job of christening the new tree. Frémont wanted his piñon
signed, sealed, and delivered in time to be included in his
official report, then in preparation. On March 23, 1845, he
wrote, "Will you not give to the Pinus Piñon the name of
your botanical friends," and on April 8, "As we cannot
make full use of our botany for the present report I only
refer slightly to the plants in the course of the narrative
. . . but I suppose it will be well to secure such as the Piñon
pine."

Torrey, meanwhile, was also concerned about the matter of a proper name. He had solicited the advice of his
former student and protégé, Asa Gray, and floated before
him the trial balloon 'Pinus Pigñon.' On Wednesday
morning, April 23, 1845, Gray responded, "My Dear Torrey: Is the spec. of Pinus Pigñon to be returned, or no? I
don't like the name Pigñon, which is not aboriginal, but
voyageur French! In haste, yours ever, A. Gray."

As Torrey procrastinated and the nomenclatural crisis
dragged on, Frémont grew more restive. On May 14, 1845,
he wrote Torrey:

> Through the narrative in using the words Pinus mono-
> phyllus, as the scientific term, I have adopted for the pop-
> ular name "Nut Pine," instead of Pigñon tree, for which
> there are good reasons. Will you not do the same.

And on May 18, with his exasperation barely controlled:

> Fearing that the remark in my last (letter) . . . may not
> have been clear to you, I think it well again to mention to
> you that I have used the words nut pine in the narrative

and that you will also use them on the plates and your "notes."

It must have been with a great sigh of relief that the impatient pathfinder later fingered copies of his published *Report of the Exploring Expedition to the Rocky Mountains in the year 1842, and to Oregon and North California in the years 1843–44*, in which a tree called the nut pine is introduced to science as *Pinus monophyllus* in the text, in the botanical appendix, and on the finely engraved plate. A technical change was later made in the ending of the species epithet, and it is known today as *Pinus monophylla* Torrey & Frémont.

The Frémont correspondence on the new piñon raises some questions too trivial for the attention of the historian but just weighty enough to be considered by curious students of botany. For example, what were those unspecified "good reasons" for adopting "Nut Pine" instead of "Pinyon tree?" And what about Professor Torrey —what were his unrecorded reactions to Frémont's feverish and frequently insulting entreaties?

First, Frémont's insistence on the name Nut Pine. Eleven years before Frémont discovered his tree for science, another had discovered it while traveling across Nevada. In 1833, a party of fur trappers under the leadership of Captain Joseph Reddeford Walker had left the trappers' rendezvous at Bear Lake in Utah and struck out for California. It was only the second attempt to reach California overland, the first having been the successful journey of Jedediah Smith and fifteen men on a southerly route in 1826. The chronicler of the Walker expedition was Zenas Leonard, a Pennsylvania farm boy seeking his fortune in the West. After crossing northern Utah, the Walker party entered Nevada. About the first week of September 1833, Leonard records a mountain now believed to be Pilot Peak, "covered with the pinone tree, bearing a kind of must (mast), which the natives are very

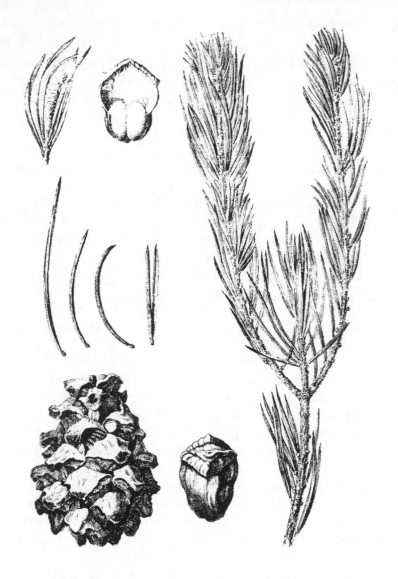

Singleleaf piñon as depicted by one of the Endicotts in Frémont's *Report* of 1845. (Engraving courtesy of Flanigan's Old Prints, Logan, Utah)

fond of, and which they collect for winter provision." Since Zenas Leonard had not been in piñon country before, it is likely that he learned the tree's name from Walker or from some other member of the party familiar with the Southwest. The piñon harvest would have been underway at the time he saw the trees, and he may have been introduced to the nuts by Indians not mentioned in his memoir. After reaching California, Leonard went back to Pennsylavania. At the urging of his neighbors, he published his diary in the local Clearfield County newspaper, and later in 1839, in book form. His mention of the piñon of the Great Basin was a casual one, with no scientific intent.

It seems likely that Frémont read Leonard's published diary before leading his own expedition, as new intelligence of the West was eagerly digested by the public. But he may not have taken special note of the tree so briefly mentioned by the young trader. Then, in the spring of 1845, while preparing his own final report, Frémont may have been reviewing the older literature and suddenly come upon the "pinone," obviously the very tree he already thought of as his own. Perhaps he felt unjustly deprived of the claim of priority in discovering the species. It may have seemed only fair that this life-sustaining tree, first appreciated by him among white men, should bear a name conferred by the serious Frémont rather than the casual Leonard. Studious avoidance of the Spanish name would allow him to present the little pine to science without having to acknowledge Leonard's prior discovery. At any rate, between April 8 and May 14, 1845, Frémont suddenly commanded that the piñon become the Nut Pine.

And John Torrey, America's foremost botanist—scientist, teacher, scholar: did he feel the sting of the pen wielded by the ambitious Major? In his correspondence with Asa Gray, there is no hint of animus toward Frémont. But one wonders whether Torrey's inner feelings influenced him in 1860 when he wrote the section on conifers for Lt. Ives's *Report on the Colorado River of the West.* In this report, Torrey identified the single-leafed piñon collected by Newberry as *Pinus edulis* var. *monophyllus* Torrey, instead of *Pinus monophyllus* Torrey & Frémont. Of course, it may have been nothing more than Torrey's considered professional opinion that the single-needle pine of the Great Basin should be regarded as a *variety* of the more recently described *Pinus edulis*; in that process, the name "Frémont" would simply drop off. On the other hand, any taxonomist will admit that delineating species and varieties is a subjective art, not an objective science, and the temperaments of many botanists have contributed to the system of plant classification and nomenclature in use today. Whatever his motives, Torrey's afterthoughts have found little support, and those who know pines today consider the singleleaf piñon a perfectly good species—by Torrey *and* Frémont.

Pinus edulis was delivered up to science by Dr. Frederick Adolphus Wislizenus, medical doctor, one-time student revolutionary, and German immigrant to southern Illinois. Wislizenus was an ardent botanist and mineralogist, and it seems natural that he became a partner to Dr. George Engelmann of St. Louis, also a German immigrant and botanist—indeed, one of the greatest students of the pine family *(Pinaceae)* up to the present day.

Unlike the sedentary Engelmann, Wislizenus had periodic fits of traveller's itch. In 1839 he accompanied an expedition to Fort Hall in the Oregon Territory during the waning days of the Rocky Mountain fur trade and witnessed the penultimate trappers' rendezvous. After a few years of doctoring, the urge came again and he joined a mercantile wagon train headed down the Santa Fe Trail. The year was 1846. Near Santa Fe, New Mexico, he collected specimens of the *pino chico* seen over three centuries earlier by Cabeza de Vaca. Of course, the tree had been seen in the interim by numerous mountain men plying the southern Rockies in pursuit of beaver, but none of them were botanists. (Some, however, were literate. And one, Warren Angus Ferris, whose life traced an arc from Glens Falls, New York, to Dallas, Texas, mentioned the nut pine in his published writings. He told how the "Sann-pitch" Indians of Utah ate the pine nuts they brought from the mountains. Ferris was in the Rockies from 1830 to 1835). To Dr. Wislizenus the piñon was new, and he surrendered his specimens to Dr. Engelmann, who christened the tree *Pinus edulis* in recognition of its "very pleasant" edible kernel.

Leaving Santa Fe, the adventurous Wislizenus headed south, into hostile territory during this year of the Mexican War. He reached Ciudad Chihuahua, Mexico, where the blood was running hot at the sight of *norteamericanos.* Wislizenus was accused of discharging a firearm in celebration of Armijo's capitulation to Doniphan at Santa Fe. He was abruptly put before a magistrate by a mob that he described as "not that short, offhand, killing affair that it is in the 'far west' of the United States; it is rather an uproarous meeting, a somewhat irregular procession, arranged with a certain decency, and executed more from love of plunder than thirst of blood." He was exiled, with other Americans, to the village of Cusihuiriachic, "a strange-looking, incomprehensible, awful place" in the Sierra Madre foothills. While interned, Wislizenus was permitted to hunt and collect plants, and among the trees whose acquaintance he made was a piñon pine with a thick, rockhard shell protecting its savory kernel. On his way home to the United States in 1847, he collected specimens of the tree, which was then described by Engelmann as *Pinus osteosperma.* But the name has passed into disuse because this tree was of the same species earlier described by Zuccarini as *Pinus cembroides,* the Mexican piñon.

Although the halcyon days of plant exploration in North America are long gone, new pines are still being discovered, and among them are members of the piñon

Colorado piñon as depicted, probably by Richard Kern, in Sit-greave's *Report* of 1853. (Engraving courtesy of Flanigan's Old Prints, Logan, Utah)

group. These include not merely newly named varieties of established species, or name changes based on differing views of what constitutes a true species: in addition to such as these, there have been recent discoveries of bona fide piñon species.

In the early 1960s, Dr. John W. Andresen, then an assistant professor of forestry at Michigan State University, was studying genetic variation in the characters of limber pine, a white pine widely distributed in the Rocky Mountains and elsewhere in the West. Andresen was routinely examining limber pine specimens filed away in various university herbaria when he was struck by a particular specimen from northern Mexico. It had been collected by an American botanist in the 1930s atop Cerro Potosí, a mountain over 12,000 feet high in the state of Nuevo León. The specimen was labeled as limber pine, but Andresen realized that, though its needles were in fascicles of five, he was looking at a piñon pine.

In 1960 Andresen and his colleague Dr. John H. Beaman headed for Cerro Potosí with high hopes: It is not every researcher who gets the opportunity to name and describe a new pine. After a long and strenuous climb, they reached the top—only to find a group of guitar-strumming Mexican picnickers who had driven up a newly built road on the other side of the mountain. They were, however, rewarded by finding a piñon growing in thick groves up to fifteen feet high. Its growth habit was typical of *Krummholz,* the low, profusely branched form assumed by windswept conifers at the timberline. It was, indeed, a piñon pine despite its high mountaintop habitat. Andresen and Beaman named it *Pinus culminicola.* Roughly translated, *culminicola* means "dweller of the mountaintop."

The five-needled piñon of Cerro Potosí was soon joined by another even more improbable piñon. For some time, rumors had circulated in Mexican forestry and botanical circles of very large pine nuts being sold in markets of

Zacatecas. In order to confirm the story, botanist Jerzy Rzedowski journeyed to the village of Juchipila, in an area of deep canyons and rugged mountains little known to outsiders. If any area could harbor a pine species still unknown to science, surely this was the place. And Rzedowski did find, in the marketplace of Juchipila, spectacularly large *piñones*, up to an inch long and as tasty as those of other *pinos piñoneros*.

The next year, in the summer of 1964, Rzedowski returned in search of the nut tree itself. In the mountains nearby, he found an area of several square kilometers, between 5,500 and 6,500 feet elevation, where scattered pines clung to the vertical walls of steep canyons. The piñons were twenty to thirty feet tall, with trunks up to a foot and a half in diameter, and their rounded crowns had a bluish cast. Rzedowski's piñon not only outdid others in seed size: its needles were twice as long as those of the other species, and its cones were up to ten inches in length. This remarkable tree was named *Pinus maximartinezii* in honor of the late Mexican botanist Maximino Martínez.

Finally, as if to complete the catalog of peculiar forms among the piñons, a new species of dwarf piñon was described in 1978, also from the state of Zacatecas. On the steep hillsides between Mazapil and the four-century-old copper mining town of Concepción del Oro, low scattered bushes of *Pinus johannis* spring from the impoverished calcareous soils, seldom reaching heights greater than ten feet. Its limited distribution on unusual soils and its proximity and resemblance in some characters to Mexican piñon suggest that it originated not very long ago as a mutant form of that species. Who knows how many more unknown piñons bake under the brassy Mexican sun? Surely some remain to be discovered.

Chapter 15

Fuel for a
Silver Empire

The production of mineral riches would not have been possible in nineteenth-century Nevada without the piñon woodlands and their vast supplies of wood. The opening of a mine was only the first of many operations necessary to convert hard rock into treasure. Huge labor forces had to be brought in to work the mines and to build and operate stamp mills, smelters, amalgamators, and concentrators. Lumber in enormous quantities was needed for these operations: timbers for shoring the mine shafts, charcoal for smelting ore, cordwood for heating and cooking. The great Nevada silver boom ran on wood. Every new Mining District was on its own at first; there were no roads or rails to bring in lumber or coal from other regions. Instead, the miners had to make the best of their local resources, and they did so with a vengeance. Here we will only scratch the surface of a historical process that has never been given its rightful share of attention: the deforestation of vast areas in the Great Basin for the production of mineral wealth.

Nevada's mining boom began with the Comstock, a great lode of silver at the western edge of the Great Basin, a few miles from the foot of the Sierra Nevada. When mining began in 1859, the mountains for miles around Virginia City were covered with piñon and juniper. These local forests were rapidly depleted. By 1868 John Ross Browne reported that the supply of local wood was "entirely exhausted," and cordwood was being brought in from Dayton, twelve miles distant. Even these woods were quickly being destroyed, and wood had to be packed in on mules from inaccessible areas back in the mountains. Piñon was selling for sixteen dollars a cord, most of the cost going for transportation. The population of the district had reached 20,000 and the daily consumption of fuelwood was 568 cords. Already it was becoming necessary to bring in wood of inferior quality from the Sierra forests.

Meanwhile, the mines of the Comstock were consuming 18 million board feet of timber annually, much of it for shorings in the tunnels. The "square-set" method of shoring mine pits, an important technological development, was also a great consumer of wood. It has been said of Virginia City that it had as much wood underground as Chicago had on the surface. In 1868 there were twenty-four sawmills operating in Nevada, producing 180,000 board feet daily.

Piñon wood makes poor lumber because it is knotty and available only in short lengths. But good boards were so expensive that piñon was used for construction material whenever possible. In Austin, deep in Central Nevada and far from the Sierran forests, lumber was brought in by teams from the Comstock Districts. In 1865 it sold for as much as $250 per thousand board feet while locally cut piñon—"Reese River lumber"—was available for $125. About half of the 2.4 million board feet of lumber used in Austin that year was Reese River piñon. Since piñon logs not suitable for lumber sold for only

Wagonloads of sacked charcoal await unloading at the Montezuma Silver and Smelting Works, Oreana, Nevada, while teamsters and their oxen take a mid-day break. The charcoal seen in this early (ca. 1868) view by Timothy O'Sullivan was probably made from piñon cut in the nearby Humboldt Range. (Photo courtesy of the National Archives)

about $6 a cord, houses were often built of short piñon logs, squared and set in the ground stockade style.

The incentive for using piñon and juniper as lumber was even greater in some other areas. At Hamilton and Treasure Hill, for example, in 1869, newly arrived miners paid premium prices for empty whiskey barrels and packing crates to build their shacks. Lt. George M. Wheeler reported to his superiors after making a reconnaissance of Nevada that there was ample "nut-pine and mountain-cedar" for fuel, but that lumber would command high prices. "This was noticed to a remarkable degree in the early days of White Pine [Mining District], when lumber was worth two hundred to three hundred dollars per thousand, allowing the shipment of it by rail from the Sierra Nevada to Elko, on the railroad, thence by freighting to White Pine with large profits." But the most important use of piñon wood—both ecologically and economically—was for production of the charcoal used in smelting ore.

In these days of electric blast furnaces, we tend to forget that metallurgy once depended on mountains of coke made from coal; and before that, on mountains of charcoal made from wood. As early as 3200 B.C., Egyptian technicians used charcoal to reduce copper ores in the Sinai. In ancient Greece, charcoal production was an important occupation that led to the wholesale cutting of forests around the copper-smelting centers of Chalke, Chalkis, and Chalkitis.

Charcoal fueled Europe's industrialization, as woodcutters stripped the forests bare in the interest of iron and glass manufacture. During the sixteenth and seventeenth centuries, enormous amounts of fine English hardwood were converted to charcoal for these purposes. The forest devastation was so serious that in 1543 Parliament prohibited the clearcutting of forest by the iron makers.

Early America also used hardwood charcoal for smelting iron ores. Eric Sloane, writing in *A Reverence for Wood*, tells how, between the Revolution and the Civil War, the hardwood trees in the Berkshires of Connecticut had been harvested every thirty-five years. The trees were "coaled," as the local people put it, in order to fire the furnaces that made three million dollars worth of Berkshire iron every year. More than half of the dollar value of that iron was in the wood that was processed into charcoal. The hardwood forest growing on sixteen square miles had to be stripped from the hills every year and turned over to the charcoal burners, strange and lonely men who carefully tended the smoking mounds of oak and maple they built among the stumps.

Those furnaces were no hungrier than others occupied with the manufacture of iron. At the beginning of this century a mammoth blast furnace in Ontario ate its way through a pile of charcoal half a mile long every twenty-four hours. It took a stack of cordwood one mile long for the charcoal needed to produce 150 tons of pig iron. And iron still depends on wood charcoal in countries where coking coal is unavailable. In 1968 a team of experts was sent by the UN's Food and Agriculture Organization to Honduras, to plan the wood harvest for an operation that would produce 50,000 tons of pig iron annually. They estimated it would take 220,000 cubic meters of pine a year, which would require clearcutting over a thousand acres of forest every month. Further south, in the Brazilian state of Minas Gerais, a massive afforestation program is projected to support iron smelting. It aims at the establishing of almost 4 million acres of eucalyptus plantations to be converted to charcoal.

The importance of charcoal lies in its efficiency as a fuel. It burns hotter than wood and produces far less waste. Thus, the profitable exploitation of Nevada's silver deposits—except the rich lodes around Virginia City, which required no smelting—depended on the availability of high-quality piñon charcoal.

It is no surprise that mining men and government agents were alert to the distribution of piñon woodland. In 1872, when Rossiter W. Raymond reported to the United States Congress on the potential of new mining districts being established in Nevada, one of his major concerns was the availability of piñon, the Great Basin's premier charcoal species. The White Pine District was well wooded and could produce dense charcoal that would "answer very well for smelting operations." He noted with approval that an abundance of piñon in the Yellow Pine District was keeping the price of firewood there to only $2.50 per cord. At Ticapoo Spring in the Tem Piute District there was enough flowing water to run a twenty-stamp mill—a rare occurrence of water power in Nevada—and plenty of nut pine and cedar for smelting.

Raymond knew the laborious efforts necessary to gather fuel in areas where there was no woodland. In the Tuscarora District, for example, vast acreages were denuded of sagebrush as enormous wagonloads of the aromatic desert shrub were hauled in and stockpiled at the mills and smelters. Sage also fueled the furnaces of Unionville, and probably those of Oreana as well, where the smelters belched smoke around the clock. In the Candelaria District, Indians were hired to cut sagebrush from the hills and pack it on burros to the mills and smelters. As the forests were scalped from the hills around Virginia City, Chinese laborers cut and hauled sagebrush to market from privately controlled "wood ranches." Mining men grew restive as they watched great tracts of woodland taken over by scheming wood merchants and their gangs of toughs. Wood was a scarce necessity of life, and the supply was up for grabs.

Charcoal was made by burning wood in airtight kilns designed to systematically and gradually exclude oxygen. A skilled coal maker learned to control the moisture content and size of the logs he put in the kiln, the rate of combustion, the burning temperature, and many other fine technical points. High-quality piñon charcoal produces about 13,000 British thermal units (Btu) per pound compared with 8,000 from the unprocessed wood. It weighs only a third as much and has but half the bulk of wood. When the early entrepreneurs of Nevada's mining industry perceived the need for charcoal and the abundance of the nut pine, they closed the circle by importing skilled Italian and Swiss-Italian *carbonari.*

Brick charcoal ovens near Tybo, Nevada. A rapidly growing young woodland of singleleaf piñon is replacing the trees that were fed into the ovens a century ago. (Photo by James A. O'Neill)

The experienced immigrant charcoal burners built their ovens of masonry or brick, or used pits in the ground that held up to a hundred cords of wood or more. They took pride in their well-honed axes and in their ability to chop a tree right down to the roots. In 1873, Rossiter Raymond described the charcoal made by Italians at Eureka, Nevada, as the best product available. It was so far superior to charcoal made in Utah, for example, that the Eureka product was being used in Little Cottonwood, just a few miles from Salt Lake City. The *carbonari* did not lack for work, as is clear from the history of coal-burning in the wooded mining districts. Let Eureka serve as an example.

Mining began in Eureka late in the 1860s, but the complex ore, containing iron, lead, antimony, and silica in addition to silver, was refractory and required new technology for profitable exploitation. In short, the days of easy silver were over, and miners had to learn to smelt their ores. Production, therefore, did not begin in earnest until the early 1870s, but within a few years such companies as the Eureka Consolidated, the Marcellina, the Phoenix, and the Richmond—some of them English-owned—had built smelters in and around Eureka. By 1873, there were thirteen smelting furnaces in operation and in 1878 there were sixteen. The amount of charcoal used to support this "Pittsburgh of the West" was staggering. The Nevada state mineralogist reported in 1873 that the thirteen Eureka furnaces had a daily capacity of 595 tons of ore. The high temperatures required for roasting Eureka ores necessitated about 30 bushels of charcoal per ton of ore; thus, if all the furnaces worked at capacity they would have consumed 17,850 bushels of charcoal daily. This is close to the figure of 16,000 bushels given by the Nevada surveyor general in his Report of 1877–78. Rossiter Raymond reported that the Eureka Consolidated consumed 4,000 bushels of charcoal a day in 1873; and the Richmond used 4,500 bushels daily in 1875. As these were apparently the largest companies in town, the figure of 16,000 bushels a day seems reasonable.

Charcoal was the biggest expense in the smelting operation, even greater than labor costs. Mining executives constantly grumbled over the prices demanded by the *carbonari*, and the smelter owners looked to a future when railroads would bring in coking coal from the vast deposits of southern Utah.

Consider the environmental impact of the smelting operation. Judge Goodwin described Eureka, in an official document of the Nevada Legislature, as a smelting camp over which rolled black clouds of dense smoke from the furnaces. These were heavily scented with fumes of lead and arsenic and were constantly depositing soot, scales, and black dust, giving Eureka the aspect of an industrial town in Pennsylvania's coal region.

But outside the city, the effects were even more severe and long lasting. A typical yield of piñon pine was ten cords per acre, and a cord made about 30 bushels of charcoal. So the furnaces of Eureka, working at capacity, could in a single day devour over 530 cords of piñon, the produce of over 50 acres. An additional 20 acres a day were being cut to provide cordwood for the mills. After one year of major activity, the hills around Eureka were bare of trees for ten miles in every direction. By 1874, the wasteland extended twenty miles from town, and by 1878 the woodland was nowhere closer than fifty miles from Eureka, every acre having been picked clean by the *carbonari* or by domestic foragers. By now the charcoal pits were being fed with logs brought in from neighboring counties, and it was a thirty-five-mile haul from the charcoal pit to the smelter. About six hundred *carbonari* were employed to supply the Eureka market.

The significance of the deforestation around Eureka can be appreciated by realizing that a fifty-mile radius from that town approaches to within a few miles of Ely to the east and of Austin to the west. Both of these towns were

Eureka, Nevada, in the early 1870s, showing the hills in the background cleared of their vegetation by charcoal burners and others who needed fuel. (Photo courtesy of Huntington Library, San Marino, California)

View of Eureka in 1978, from the same vantage point, showing the new growth of singleleaf piñon woodland. (Photo by Harriette Lanner)

also important mining centers with large populations, and their demands for woodland products probably rivaled those of Eureka itself.

Even in the isolated Delamar District of southeastern Nevada, which was a relatively small one-company operation, contracts as large as ten thousand cords were let. Woodcutters and their families moved into the woodlands, migrating further from the smelter as the hills were cleaned off. Wood was brought in from as much as fifty miles away, packed in on roads built by woodsmen.

The deforestation of their hills and the destruction of their nut groves often brought Indians into conflict with white settlers and miners. As early as 1860, Paiutes gathered at Pyramid Lake to decide how to cope with the white men who were encroaching on their lands, killing their game, and cutting down what the settlers derisively referred to as the Indians' "orchards."

Violence connected with the felling of the nut pines cropped up elsewhere in Nevada as well. In 1863, Henry E. Herter was killed on the Gould & Curry wood ranch near Steamboat Springs "by parties unknown." In 1869, John L. Roach was murdered by Frank Rankin during a dispute over wood sales in Pine Nut Valley. A Chinese laborer was killed on a wood ranch in Diamond Valley in 1876, and the following year at Mackay & Fair's wood camp near Reno a man named McDonald slew one called Murray.

In May of 1876, the Two G Mining Company of Tybo contracted with a group of charcoal burners for a large quantity of piñon charcoal. The contractors then brought in Chinese workers to cut the trees and fire the kilns. An irate mob of night riders, organized as the Anti-Asiatic League of Tybo, attacked the Chinese with gunfire and bullwhips, forcing them to work with armed guards posted in the woodland. Finally, the Chinese left Tybo, their stage fares paid by their antagonists. In 1879, a few miles to the north, near Eureka, a far more serious episode occurred. Ever since smelting began in Eureka, the operators had chafed under the heavy cost of fuel. In 1873, Rossiter Raymond quoted a letter from W. S. Keyes, superintendent of the Eureka Consolidated Mining Company, that the ever-diminishing supply of piñon wood was forcing up the price of charcoal. Already Eureka Consolidated was paying $40 a ton to satisfy "the grasping aspirations of the coal-burners." Between July 1870 and September 1871, the Consolidated spent over a quarter of a million dollars for charcoal. At first, charcoal sold for 30 cents a bushel, but the price was going up. Raymond attacked 33-cents-a-bushel charcoal as "threatening the very life of the industry." Actually, lower prices than that prevailed over the next few years. By 1879, the Consolidated was paying 25 to 26½ cents, and by then it was the *carbonari,* who earned less than half as much as mine laborers, who were chafing. Meanwhile, the Eureka Coal Burners Association had been formed for the purpose of raising the price of charcoal to 30 cents. The strife that followed culminated at Fish Creek, about twenty miles south of Eureka, on the evening of August 18, 1879, when five *carbonari* were shot to death by a sheriff's posse.

But, as is usual in Western history, it was the Indians who lost the most when the woods were stripped from their hills. David Hurst Thomas has described the positive feedback system—or vicious circle—in which the Shoshone found themselves around Austin, Nevada. The mining and urban activities there required huge amounts of wood, and the burgeoning population consumed prodigious amounts of food. Local Indians helped provide both of these commodities by working for wages as lumberjacks and ranch hands. Those who cut down trees were destroying the source of their traditional winter food, pine nuts. Those who punched cattle aided and abetted the eradication of the native grasses that provided their traditional summer fare of grass seed. The more these food sources were destroyed, the more dependent the

Indians became on wages; and the more they engaged in lumbering and ranching for white men, the more they destroyed their food sources. By the time the bubble burst in the 1880s and 1890s when the mining industry collapsed, the piñon groves were gone, the valley grasslands were fenced for cattle, and much of the old culture was forsaken.

CHAPTER 16

Turning Woodlands Into Pastures
The Hard Way

The clearcutting of piñon woodland in the Great Basin slowed with the near demise of the mining industry in late nineteenth-century Nevada, but it did not end. During the 1920s and 1930s there was a brief revival of silver mining, and again piñon trees became a locally valuable resource. When the smelter at Tonopah reopened, it created a need for trees growing on lands of the Toiyabe National Forest, and for a time timber sales on the Tonopah Ranger District outdid those of any district in the Forest Service's Intermountain Region.

At about the same time, farmers were eyeing the woodlands of the southwestern corner of Colorado, where the deep red soils promised heavy yields of pinto beans. Foresters of the time argued strenuously that the highest use of those woodlands was as forest, producing fuelwood, fence posts, and pine nuts for the sparse population inhabiting that high dry plateau. The foresters were outvoted by economic needs, and the area between Cortez and the Utah border was cleared of woodland and put to the plow. Today Dove Creek, Colorado, is the pinto bean "capital" of the world, and enormous crops of pinto beans are harvested from about a fifth of a million acres of those rolling lands. Woodland remnants are still found in places where the soil is thin, steep, or rocky, but from the foot of Mesa Verde to the breaks of Montezuma Creek the pinto bean is king. Downhill plowing and careless management still result in heavy soil erosion on many of those farms, but the economic and nutritional benefits of bean growing seem to have vindicated the agriculturists of half a century ago.

A less convincing program of woodland clearing began, however, in the 1950s. This time the woodland was viewed as a gigantic potential pasture for the grazing of cattle. Of course, since the earliest white settlement, accessible tracts of woodland had always been grazed. Overgrazing and timber trespass had, in fact, combined to make the woodland one of the worst-abused vegetation types in the West: even now, the acre of woodland where one can find refuge from the ubiquitous cow pat is a rarity. But as the post-World War II hunger for red meat mounted, the Forest Service started carving up National Forest woodlands with bulldozers and chains, hoping to create greener pastures for white men's buffalo.

"Chaining" is done by attaching the ends of a battleship anchor chain to two crawler tractors which then drive parallel to each other, dragging the chain through the woodland, uprooting the trees in their path. After the trees are piled or scattered, the area is seeded with forage plants, usually crested wheatgrass, a native of central Asia. Burning, herbicide spraying, and tree felling are also practiced; in Arizona and New Mexico the Forest Service has used the eighty-ton "Tree Crusher" to drive through the woodland, the blades on its electrically powered wheels riding over the trees and chopping them into firewood-sized chunks. Reliable figures are hard to come by, but it is estimated that between 1950 and 1964 three million acres of woodland were converted to pasture. Between 1960 and 1972, over a third of a million acres were chained by the Forest Service and the Bureau of Land Management (BLM) in Utah and Nevada alone.

When chaining began, there were numerous protests from concerned citizens, but the powerful environmental movement had not yet come of age, and no serious organized opposition appeared. Still, the heavy-handedness of the technique, its drastic effects on the landscape, and its apparent lack of benefit for anyone—except holders of cattle leases on public land—should open the program to skepticism, if not to attack.

According to the Forest Service, chaining is a plant control program, intended to "rehabilitate" millions of acres of land that were historically grassland, or shrubland, but where the woodland has "invaded." The Forest Service asserts that the woodland is aggressively moving in, thus devaluing good rangeland. Range managers express puzzlement over whether the woodland's alleged advance is due to overgrazing, fire protection on lands once subject to periodic burning, or even climatic change. While the concept of a massive, regionwide invasion is offered as justification for wholesale uprooting of piñon and juniper trees, the validity of the invasion hypothesis remains undemonstrated and open to serious challenge.

To validate the invasion hypothesis two things are essential. First, it must be shown that a given tract of land was in grass or shrubs up to the time it was settled; and second, that it later became wooded. The Forest Service has published "before and after" photographs in which the earlier photograph records the vegetation during the settlement period. These photographs show extensive treeless areas in the hills around villages, with woodland present only on the distant mountains. But that is not satisfactory evidence of virgin grassland or shrubland. These old photographs may simply record deforested

Large chained areas of piñon-juniper woodland on the Carson National Forest, New Mexico. (Photo by U.S. Forest Service, Southwestern Region)

Chained woodland on the Wasatch National Forest in north-central Utah. (Photo by the author)

slopes already stripped for lumber, posts, firewood, and other necessities of early rural life.

Until the extent of early deforestation has been established, it will not be possible to determine whether young stands of piñon and juniper (up to a hundred years or so of age) constitute an invasion into new territory or simply the reestablishment of woodland on its former sites. This is especially true of Nevada, where historical evidence clearly demonstrates that clearcutting was widespread over a period of decades.

Although the Forest Service proposes an invasion hypothesis, its actual practice is curiously inconsistent with its theory. If it were simply dedicated to the restoring of invaded lands, it might be expected to chain only those areas where invasion was known to have occurred. But no inventory of such lands has ever been made, and no map exists that pinpoints invasions. Apparently, the lands that go under the chain are selected not because there is evidence that they were invaded, but because they are convenient. Thus, while the Forest Service justifies its program as a necessary measure to control an invading forest, it has routinely applied the method to old stands that were present long before settlement.

What do the Forest Service and BLM hope to achieve by chaining? Quite a bit, if their claims are taken at face value. Chaining is said to increase livestock forage, reduce erosion, increase water yield by allowing more runoff to feed into river systems, increase the mule deer herd, protect trees from insects and disease, preserve the rural health and economy, and much more. Unfortunately, these claims cannot be taken at face value.

While livestock forage usually does increase after removal of tree cover—if investments are made in cultivating and seeding the cleared land—seldom do the economic benefits justify the costs of chaining incurred by the Treasury. It was not until the chaining program was in its third decade that the Forest Service started to analyze its economics. In a comprehensive cost-benefit study made in 1974, Forest Service economists concluded that "the more successful conversion projects just about break even from a benefit-cost standpoint." Another Forest Service study, conducted by staff members rather than researchers, predicted that chaining would add to the economy $1.08 for every dollar invested in the program and that most of the benefit would be due to increased livestock production. But they assumed that once an area is chained, the trees would not come back for fifty years.

Such an assumption was mere speculation, for chaining had only been done for about twenty-five years at that time. In fact, many chained areas have required additional expensive clearing after only fifteen to twenty years, with clearing costs as high as seventy dollars per acre. And the cost of chaining has undoubtedly increased since the 1973 oil embargo because tractor operating expenses are a major factor. The Forest Service may be right about chaining making increased forage yields possible, but such yields cannot be expected to do more than repay the cost of producing them—and then only in the best situations. The poor economic performance of chained pastures has recently been verified by independent research.

According to Forest Service advocates of chaining, piñon trees shade understory plants which then die, leaving the soil subject to erosion. By removing the trees and establishing a cover of grass and forbs, they believe that erosion can be reduced. They also reason that removal of the deep-rooted trees will make more water available for downstream water users. Unfortunately, neither benefit has been borne out by hydrologic research. A 1974 study, again by Forest Service scientists, concluded that water quality and sediment yields—indicators of erosion—were not significantly affected by chaining and that water yields were not likely to be increased. When the argument that chaining improves the watershed is not even borne out by the Forest Service's own research, the similar negative conclusions of independent scientists seem almost redundant.

The Forest Service also considers wildlife, especially the mule deer herd, a major beneficiary of woodland eradication. Mule deer use the piñon-juniper woodland heavily as winter range, and the idea favored by chaining advocates is that openings in the tree cover provide needed deer forage. Again, research results by Forest Service scientists in Arizona and New Mexico, and by others in

Utah, Colorado, and Nevada, uniformly fail to support this position. Numerous studies agree that chaining does not result in increases either in the deer herd, in the hunter's take, or in the supposed concomitant benefits to the rural economy.

Deer do not benefit from the increased forage produced in extensive chained areas, for one thing, because of their hesitancy to expose themselves in large openings. Many chained clearings are hundreds or even thousands of acres in size. To enhance their value for deer, chainings would have to be small in size. In other words, if chaining is intended to improve deer habitat, it should be done by "punching" small holes in the woodland matrix, not by leaving wooded "islands" to provide cover in large cleared areas. But chaining done in this way scatters the increased forage widely, depriving the stockman of the concentrated pasturing areas he desires, and greatly increasing the per-acre cost of clearings.

Why do the Forest Service and BLM go to great lengths to justify a program shown to be uneconomic and destructive of a major natural vegetation type? The answer may lie partly in the sociology of government bureaucracies, and partly in the special interests of the people involved.

Chaining is popular among livestockmen, since they are the ones who reap its benefits. Stockmen are politically influential in the Western states, and Western congressmen are sympathetic towards them. So it is not surprising that chaining programs in national forests and BLM districts have traditionally met with congressional approval in the form of appropriations from the Treasury. Many Forest Service and BLM personnel are technically trained as range managers and naturally identify with their client cattlemen, whose concern is the profitable production of red meat and to whom woodland is an impediment. Some of the cattlemen who lease public grazing lands do not always live up to their contractual obligations. The pros-

pect of having some of their leaseholds chained has sometimes been dangled before them, by federal range
managers, as an incentive to do right. Finally, woodlands
are relatively unproductive forests, and have long posed
vexing management problems for commodity-oriented
foresters. Consequently, they are classified as non-com-
mercial forest. Turning them into pastures is easier than
figuring out how to manage them as forests. For these
reasons chaining has aroused the support, and even the
enthusiasm, of many federal agency land managers.

The desirability of chaining could be gauged on its
economic impact alone. What is the logic of destroying
millions of acres of natural vegetative cover at a cost in
excess of the benefits? Meanwhile, this hidden subsidy of
the livestock industry is borne by all the taxpayers. As
new trees seed into the clearings—the piñon jays that
plant piñons and the thrushes that defecate juniper seeds
will see to it that they do—the agencies may again cry
"invasion!" And then there will be pressure to throw good
money after bad to reclear the same old clearings.

The most permanent damage caused by chaining is the
large-scale demolition of countless archeological sites. As
the home of most of the Southwest's early Indian cultures, the woodland is a treasure-trove of prehistoric artifacts, *in situ,* on and just beneath the surface. A Forest
Service archeologist assessing the damage done by chains
and pirouetting crawler tractors has pointed out that "ad-
verse site impacts from chaining might . . . accurately be
estimated as nearly 100 percent." These sites represent an
unrenewable national cultural resource that still awaits
full development by students of American prehistory. It
is ironic that their destruction is underway by agencies
charged with their protection under the Antiquities Act of
1906. A citizen who removes an arrowhead or smashes an
ancient clay pot on these lands is subject to arrest and
imprisonment by a federal magistrate. But the taxpayers
pay to have the job done wholesale.

Finally, chaining has been an unmitigated disaster for many Western Indians. The Northern Paiutes and Western Shoshones of Nevada have in recent years become radicalized by confrontation with the federal agencies, especially BLM, via their outrage at seeing trees they hold sacred and rely on for a traditional diet ripped from the earth for the benefit of white men's cattle. Bad enough, in their eyes, to see out-of-state commercial nut dealers given exclusive harvesting permits in some favored areas; worse yet to be themselves charged money to harvest pine nuts in excess of twenty-five pounds; but worst of all to see the trees that produce their most valued food destroyed by their own government.

CHAPTER 17

Tomorrow's Woodland

What future has the woodland? Since the arrival of white settlers in the Southwest the woodland has felt the impact of fire, grazing, clearing, and accelerated erosion. More impacts can be expected in the near future as urbanization proceeds and energy development increases.

Man is returning to the land of piñons and junipers. Some towns, like Santa Fe and Taos, New Mexico, use their environment sympathetically. Many others achieve the look of a universal subdivision by flattening the low native forest and replacing it with store-bought trees.

The Southwest is becoming a very popular place for the generation of electric power, mainly for the metropolitan inhabitants of Los Angeles and Phoenix, and the likelihood of widespread growth impacts on the native vegetation cannot be dismissed. Coal-fired power plants may be damaging to woodland vegetation as their sulfur dioxide fumes pollute the heretofore clear Southwestern skies. Piñon pines are related to the white pines, which have

already been found highly susceptible to both sulfur dioxide and ozone.

Strip mining of coal will wipe out many forested acres
in the Hopi country and perhaps eventually on the
Kaiparowits Plateau; as the oil-bearing shales of Utah and
Colorado become economically usable, a further fraction
of woodland will disappear. Though land reclamation
efforts will necessarily be made, the reconstitution of
woodland may prove time-consuming if not impossible.

Chaining will probably continue, regardless of its
diseconomies and destructiveness, either until an out-
raged public demands a halt or until the public lands
agencies rediscover in themselves a sense of informed
professionalism. The Southwestern Region of the Forest
Service (in Arizona and New Mexico) is already starting
a woodland management program that looks beyond the
stockman's interests. If other administrative units follow
suit, a new day may yet dawn in federally managed
woodlands.

Some acres may suffer a fate even worse than chaining.
In 1974, foresters in California and Nevada developed a
scheme to chain woodland, grind the trees into chips to
be shipped to Japan, and plant grass on the cleared land.
Their plan was to try this on Indian reservation lands
since, by so doing, they could avoid the environmental
impact statement the law requires on other federal lands.

Throughout the United States, we are urbanizing and
industrializing our agricultural and forest lands at a rapid
pace, thus jeopardizing our ability to fill future needs. As
our land base further dwindles, increasing controversy
and contest will undoubtedly arise over the use of public
lands in the West. Greater pressure than ever before will
be exerted on the woodland, by utilitarian interests on the
one hand, and by environmental partisans on the other.
Stockmen will claim the woodland as a potential range
resource worthy of intensive development—at federal expense—and will demand more roads, more fences, more

water development. Their critics will respond with pleas to save the woodland and preserve large areas of it in a wild state, unfenced, unchained, and with fewer cows. They will point to the results of past abuses and object to public subsidy of further destructive practices on these public lands.

The woodland may be big enough to fulfill both these visions, to a degree, and others as well. Not all piñon-juniper land is the same: some is steep and rocky, some is on broad flat mesa tops, and some is on broken rolling foothills. Productivity likewise varies. Where soils are deep and topography relatively flat, it may be feasible to graze cattle and to harvest forest products simultaneously without materially reducing the productivity of the land.

Maintaining the land's capacity to make grass and shrubs and trees and animals—that is the essential ingredient that has been missing in past woodland management. And that is what must be kept uppermost in the minds of future public land managers: the difference between exploitation and careful husbandry. A woodland no longer abused will slowly regain the productivity ultimately determined by the quality of its soil, the salubriousness of its climate, and the biological capacities of its plants. In such a woodland there will be many management options. The unsubsidized production of beef and wood products on a nondestructive basis is only feasible on land where yields are high and accessibility is good. Such tracts may be able to support the production of several joint products that are not mutually exclusive. For example, on woodland of high site quality it might be economically feasible to graze some cattle while producing forest products. The latter might include juniper fence posts, always in demand in the West; pine nuts; piñon charcoal; firewood; and Christmas trees. All of this has been done for many years, but on an ad hoc basis, not as the result of long-term planning to preserve or raise productivity.

Trees protect the land and moderate its climate. When, in addition to their ameliorative qualities, they also produce food for man or his livestock, we cannot afford to neglect them. In 1950, geographer J. Russell Smith published *Tree Crops—A Permanent Agriculture,* his visionary yet practical program for integrating trees and woodlands into agriculture on a grand scale. Smith showed that greatly increased food productivity could result from the planting and culturing of nut and fruit trees on marginal lands. Some of the trees he advocated growing would be used for man's food, but others, notably the oaks, would produce livestock food. Smith presented many examples of trees capable of outproducing conventional crop plants while protecting the soil fertility so quickly depleted under cropping.

Smith's ideas have had small impact in this country, where agriculture is highly mechanized and where the use of a man's time has always been taken more seriously than the use of his land. But we must start to take land more seriously because the amount we are using coincides closely now with what we have. Each year, more and more prime agricultural land is converted into highways, airfields, housing developments, and truck stops. Meanwhile, both population and the need for foreign exchange continue to climb. Perhaps it is time to exhume Smith's great vision and evaluate the prospects for harvesting acorns, chestnuts, honey-locust and mesquite pods, persimmons, mulberries, walnuts, and hickory nuts on a vast scale from woodland trees, roadside trees, yard trees, and shade trees.

And why not the piñon? Millions of acres of woodland are already in place in the Southwest, the trees adapted to the climate, established, and producing. Very large areas of gentle topography lie along paved roads. They present an opportunity that has never been taken advantage of on a large scale. Their productivity—in terms of pine-nut protein, fat, and starch—is unknown and unresearched, but it may in many areas far exceed the red meat these same lands can produce. Back in 1920, forester Walter Perry estimated the piñon crop in a part of New Mexico at three hundred pounds per acre. After shelling, excluding all but the protein, and assuming such a crop occurs only once in six years, that still comes to an average annual production of over four pounds of protein per acre. There is no way at present to judge the applicability of these figures to other areas throughout the woodland, and such research is badly needed.

Though J. Russell Smith's ideas about tree crops have made little headway here in his homeland, progress can be reported from overseas. Toyohiko Kajawa popularized "forest farming" in Japan, where eroded hill farms were reforested with walnut trees, and the walnuts fed to pigs that provided a cash income for the farmers. The idea spread also to southern Africa, where forester J. Sholto Douglas introduced "three-dimensional forestry" in the 1950s. Douglas's concepts received the attention of UNESCO and have recently been presented in his book *Forest Farming.*

In a world of swelling populations and a shrinking land base, can we afford *not* to consider the alternative of using some of our best and most accessible woodlands for the production of high-grade vegetable protein and oil? To ignore this enormous resource would be folly. A recent research report prepared for the National Science Foundation evaluates a large number of native plants for potential use as new crops in the United States. Piñon is one of twenty such plants whose production is seen as primary in terms of benefits to the national economy.

Piñon "farms" would be unusual, but not unique. In Mediterranean Europe and North Africa, the Italian stone pine *(Pinus pinea)* has long been cultivated for its nuts. Familiarity with this species prepared the early *conquis-*

tadores for the sight of Indians picking pine nuts. In Spain the *piñones* grace numerous recipes and are a highly esteemed confection.

Pine nuts are gathered on a large scale in the Soviet Union from the Siberian stone pine *(Pinus sibirica)*. This slow-growing tree forms dense forests throughout a vast area extending east of the Urals and across the Siberian uplands. The nuts are gathered by industrial collectives and sent to factories where the oil is pressed from them. Trees are grown in plantations around Ural villages to produce not lumber, but seed crops. In recent years, Soviet forestry researchers have started improvement programs aimed at providing genetically superior planting stock of this species. There is no technical reason why piñons could not also be successfully cultivated, or managed in improved wild stands, given suitable economic conditions.

The tending of woodland tracts for pine-nut protein production would allow for other uses as well. Thinning of trees to maximize the nut crop would also yield fuelwood and posts. Deer could continue to use the woodlands since they cause no damage to the potential nut crop. Similarly, recreational use of the woodland need not be seriously affected by forest farming operations. The needs of native wildlife would, of course, have to be given high priority, to assure them the pine nuts they require.

Piñon trees could contribute important benefits not only in the American Southwest, but in other semiarid lands as well. The large number of piñon species and their occurrence in different climatic zones suggest that a piñon could be found for almost any dry-forest zone in the temperate or subtropical world. *Monophylla* and *edulis* are frost hardy. The former is adapted to Mediterranean climates with dry summers and wet winters, while the latter is adapted to summer-rainfall areas. Mexican piñon is widespread in subtropical areas with spring or summer rainfall in varying amounts. All these species are reservoirs of great genetic variability, allowing enormous scope for crop-breeding programs. Theoretically, there is no reason why piñon trees could not someday clothe the now-barren slopes of the Atlas Mountains or the Troodos; the Lebanons or the Judean Hills; the highlands of Anatolia or the edges of the Rajasthan Desert. The New World has already presented many gifts of new foods to the Old: the time may be ripe for one more.

Pine-Nut Cookery

by Harriette Lanner

Next morning we were off betimes with the infantry; the
scenery all day was wild, and strange to us; bare of trees
or grass,—save on the ridges where cedars and pines were
to be seen . . . near noon, a good spring was found, and
there we passed several hours under the shade of *piñón*
trees, indulging in lunch, with claret wine and *piñón* nuts
for dessert.

August 3, 1846

> Philip St. George Cooke
> Captain, First Dragoons
> Army of the West

In the spring we would collect lots of young crickets when
they are young. We used to mash them and dry them
between stones and eat them in pine-nut soup. That's
very rich food.

March 16, 1978

> Gladys Williams
> Battle Mountain, Nevada

Going Pine Nutting

Throughout the long, hot, Southwestern summer, the woodland is a lonely place, frequented by few visitors. But when the frosty mornings and sunny afternoons of Indian summer arrive, it can become a busy place indeed, Rural natives of piñon country—especially Indians and Hispanic Americans—have always made pine nutting an important fall activity, and today many urbanites are finding it an enjoyable recreational activity with dietary benefits. As a result, highways through choice stretches of piñon woodland can look like linear parking lots when a bumper crop of *piñones* is ready for harvest.

Following is a list of hints for those who are new to this pastime or would like to improve their style.

Where to go: Pine nuts can be collected most easily on public lands in New Mexico, Arizona, Colorado, Utah, Nevada, and California. You should check with local offices of the Bureau of Land Management (U.S. Department of Interior) or Forest Service (U.S. Department of Agriculture) for information on where there is a harvestable crop. These agencies sometimes issue news releases to make such information public, and their field personnel can direct you to productive areas. Permits and payment are not normally required except for commercial pickers. Many pine nutters, when they have a choice, prefer to go where they can find the richer, oilier, more flavorful *edulis* nuts; but then there are more practical folk who favor the regions where they can find the thinner-shelled *monophylla* nuts with their larger kernels.

When to go: Pine nuts are always ripe by Labor Day, though the cones may just be starting to open. The larger the crop, the longer the harvesting season; in a good year, nuts will be available into November, and in an exceptional year (like 1978 in parts of Nevada) nuts will still litter the ground the next spring.

What to take: If you are going to leave the paved road, a map is essential, as are the first aid supplies and water jug of all prudent Western travelers. To be safe, make sure you include a snakebite kit. Wear your oldest clothes, so you won't shy away from pitchy trees, and strong boots. The only specialized equipment you'll need is a six-to-twelve-foot pole with a hook on the end, an old sheet or blanket, and a bunch of old boxes or burlap gunnysacks.

How to get the nuts: The method of harvesting depends on whether the cones are still green and tightly closed or have already opened up. If cones are closed, pull branches down with your hooked pole and remove the cones by "unscrewing" until they come loose. Then release the branch and put the cones into your gunny sack. Bring several sacks, because the green cones are heavy and you'll want to distribute the weight. Some pine nutters favor ladders so they can get the higher cones, but a little walking around will provide plenty of cones within easy reach. Green cones can best be opened by spreading them out indoors, as in a basement, where they open uniformly in about a week. Despite popular myth, a freeze is not necessary to open the cones: the scales are forced open by tissue shrinkage resulting from slow drying out. When they have opened, you can extract the nuts by tapping the cones or vigorously shaking them in a box or sack. The pile of dried cones you will have accumulated need not be thrown out with the trash, but can be kept as fireplace tinder. As they burn, the pitch encrusting their scales will bubble and ignite, filling your room with incense.

If the cones have already opened, you may want to pick the fallen nuts off the ground. In most areas, good nuts are dark chocolate in color and empty ones are tan, so avoid the tan ones unless your own experimenting shows they are filled. If you don't like crawling about on your knees, you can spread a sheet or blanket under a tree and shake the branches or strike them with a pole. Or you can hold a shallow basket or shoe box under the cones as you gently tap them with a short stick. While you are at it, you may also want to pick ripe chokecherries and Oregon grapes, which mature at about the same time as *piñones*.

If you go pine nutting, and especially if you pick green cones, your hands are going to become so sticky that all five fingers will feel like one. Don't use strong solvents like turpentine, kerosene, or acetone to cut the pitch. Instead, use commercial "waterless hand cleaner," cooking oil, or, if you have water with which to rinse, borax powder.

Some other "don'ts:"

Don't break or cut down branches to get cones, or commit the crowning, inexcusable folly of cutting down the tree. "Unscrew" the cone gently and it will come off with minimal damage to the branch that bears it. When in the woodland, behave as if it were your neighbor's orchard. It is.

Don't raid squirrel caches. In 1977, members of a Mormon congregation in southern Utah were roundly criticized in the press because they sold plundered nuts as a church fund-raiser. Rodents work for their pine nuts, and you should work for yours. A peculiarly just fate might befall the robber of rodent hoards: recently, fleas have transmitted the once-dreaded bubonic plague from infected rodents to hapless people in several areas of the West. Avoid rodent caches, and you'll minimize your chances of encountering a stray flea.

Storing

In order to store freshly collected pine nuts for any length of time, two points must be observed: first, keep them in the shell; and second, keep them dry and ventilated. Pack them in cloth or paper bags in a cool, well-ventilated area, and piñons will keep for two or three years with few nuts turning rancid. If fresh piñons, high in moisture content, are stored in tightly closed jars they will soon mold, but after they have "cured," or partially dried, they can be safely closed up. Freezer storage is also feasible, and frozen piñons will keep almost indefinitely.

Fresh piñons, right from the tree, have plump, moist, white kernels. As they cure, the kernels shrink from the walls of the seed coat and harden. If properly stored they will retain this condition and be ready for shelling and roasting.

Shelling

Shelling is not much fun, but several methods can be tried. We have used a rolling pin to crack nuts spread on a breadboard and covered with a dish towel. Go easy in order not to mash the kernels. Or you can pound the covered nuts with the end of a glass jar, with practice learning to strike with just the right amount of force— enough to crack the shells, but not enough to smash the kernels. If the piñons are too dried out, they will be brittle and it will be difficult to remove them whole from the cracked shell.

The most elegant method we've tried simulates the behavior of a piñon jay or nutcracker. Set the jaws on a pair of adjustable vise-jaw pliers to a spacing somewhat tighter than the smallest pine nuts in the lot. Then grip each nut separately and close the jaws down sharply. Slowly but surely, you'll build a heap of neatly cracked piñons that can easily be shelled without injuring the meats.

Each kernel contains a rodlike yellow structure buried within the white endosperm tissue. This is the embryo that would have become a seedling if the seed had germinated. If you look closely you will see about half a dozen miniature needles in a tuft at one end.

Something to remember if you plan to snack on piñons: *Monophylla* nuts have very thin shells that are easily cracked in the fingers. *Edulis* nuts have thicker shells and will require the use of your teeth. The Mexican piñons eaten just south of the border have very thick shells that should be cracked with pliers, never with your teeth.

Roasting

Pine nuts can be eaten raw, but roasting is necessary to bring out their full flavor. They can be roasted in or out of the shell. Some prefer to keep them in a hot oven for a short time—like 450°F for 10 minutes—while others favor an hour or two at 250°. Actually the time and temperature will depend on how much moisture is still in the nuts—the more moisture, the longer the nuts take to roast. Spread some in a cookie tin or roasting pan and experiment. Be careful not to scorch them. Roasted nuts can be safely stored in closed jars.

Pine-Nut Recipes

These recipes call for pine nuts that have been shelled and roasted. They are but a sampling of the international pine-nut cuisine of Europe, North Africa, Asia, and North America. Pine nuts are also used widely for thickening soups, garnishing ice cream, and making fruit and vegetable salads of many kinds. Take these recipes as suggestions, and create your own uses for this versatile and nutritious product of pine forests the world over.

Salads, Sauces, Dressings

Avocado-Piñon Appetizer (Robert West Howard)

2 ripe avocados
Juice of 1 lemon
Juice of 1 lime (or ½ orange)
½ cup chopped pine nuts
1 firm tomato, cored, cubed, and drained on paper toweling
3 scallions, sliced thin (include tops)
½ clove garlic, peeled and crushed
¼ teaspoon crushed coriander seed
¼ teaspoon fresh ground pepper
1 teaspoon Worcestershire sauce
¼ teaspoon Tabasco sauce
¼ teaspoon salt
Pimiento slivers (garnish)
Parsley or watercress sprigs (garnish)

Halve avocados, remove seeds; scoop out flesh and mix with lemon and lime juices. Put through a food mill or puree in a blender. Combine with all remaining ingredients except the garnishes. Fill the four avocado shells. Garnish with pimiento slivers and sprigs of parsley or watercress. Serve as an appetizer or salad.

Pine-nut Salad Dressing

¾ cup pine nuts, coarsely chopped
½ teaspoon tarragon
⅛ teaspoon nutmeg
¼ teaspoon grated lemon peel
⅓ cup vinegar
½ cup salad oil
½ teaspoon salt

Blend the ingredients thoroughly and serve on any green salad.

Pine-nut Salad (Robert West Howard)

3 large cucumbers, peeled and diced
1 cup finely sliced celery
Small bunch parsley, minced
1 cup coarsely chopped olives
2 cups shredded raw spinach
1 cup pine nuts

Dressing: 2 parts olive oil
           1 part vinegar
           Salt and pepper
           Pinch of oregano

Pine-nut Sauce

½ cup pine nuts, chopped
½ teaspoon sugar, or to taste
Salt to taste
2 tablespoons lemon juice
1 teaspoon jalapeño pepper, finely chopped
½ cup parsley

Combine ingredients and serve over vegetables, meat, or seafood.

Pine-nut Spaghetti Sauce

⅓ cup watercress, finely chopped
1 clove garlic, mashed
2 ounces butter
⅓ cup pine nuts
⅓ cup grated cheese (parmesan or romano)
⅛ teaspoon salt
¼ to ⅓ cup oil

Place pine nuts, garlic, watercress, and salt in blender and puree the mixture. Add cheese and gradually mix in the oil and butter. Serve over spaghetti.

Pesto (Robert West Howard)

2 cups basil leaves
1 cup roasted pine nuts
4 cloves garlic
1½ cups parmesan cheese
1½ cups olive oil

Blend in a blender or pound in a mortar the basil, nuts, and garlic until they form a thick puree. Add the cheese and oil slowly, blending constantly until the mixture reaches a creamy consistency.

The pesto may be used on baked potatoes or spaghetti or as a base for various sauces and dressings.

Main Dishes

Stuffed Eggplant

3 eggplants
1 12-oz. can tomato puree

Stuffing: 1 pound ground lamb
½ pound butter
1 onion, chopped
½ cup pine nuts
Dash of allspice, nutmeg, and cinnamon
Salt and pepper to taste

Sauté lamb and onion in butter. Remove from skillet and brown pine nuts in butter. Remove from butter and mix together all stuffing ingredients.

Skin eggplant. Cut in quarters lengthwise. Sauté in butter. Place side by side in baking dish. Slit pieces in center and stuff each piece with 1 tablespoon of stuffing. Pour tomato puree (thinned with a little water) over the eggplant. Bake at 350° for 20 minutes.

Stuffed Cabbage

1 medium-sized cabbage
1 cup rice
1 pound lean ground beef
1 egg
1 onion
¾ cup pine nuts
¾ cup sugar or to taste
1 15-oz. can of tomato sauce

Combine ground beef, egg, pine nuts, onion, and rice. Steam the cabbage in a large saucepan (cover with water) until leaves are slightly tender. Remove the cabbage from the saucepan and cool. Carefully remove the leaves from the cabbage. Place 2 to 3 tablespoons of meat mixture on each leaf and roll up. Place the rolled cabbage leaves in a large saucepan and cover with the tomato sauce and sugar. Cook until the cabbage is tender.

Halibut Genoa

2 pounds halibut
¼ cup olive oil
2 medium-sized garlic cloves
½ cup pine nuts
¼ cup minced parsley
1 pound canned tomatoes
1 chopped onion

Cover fish with ¼ teaspoon salt. Rub a baking dish with olive oil; place salted fish in dish. Fry the pine nuts and garlic cloves in the rest of the olive oil until lightly browned, then remove to bowl and mash to a paste. Sauté onions in olive oil. Gradually add parsley and 1 teaspoon of olive oil to the garlic and nut paste; mix until it forms a smooth greenish paste. Add tomatoes to the cooked onions and simmer 5 minutes. Add the parsley paste. Add salt and pepper to taste and cover fish with sauce.

Bake at 350° for ½ hour. Serves 6.

Venetian Fillet of Sole

2 pounds fillet of sole
3 teaspoons salt
2 teaspoons pepper
2 tablespoons flour
1 cup olive oil
1 cup chopped zucchini
2 medium onions, finely chopped
1 cup diced celery
2 bay leaves, crushed
¼ cup raisins
½ cup pine nuts
¾ cup white wine vinegar
1¾ cups dry white wine
1 tablespoon olive oil
1 tablespoon raisins

Pound the fillets of sole until very thin, and cut into strips 8 inches long by 1 inch wide. Mix the salt, pepper, and flour and lightly cover each strip of sole on both sides. Heat the cup of olive oil in a large skillet, place the sole in the skillet, and cook for 1 minute on each side over medium heat. Remove the strips of sole, drain on paper towels, and place in a large shallow bowl. To the pan juices add 1 tablespoon olive oil, 2 tablespoons salt, zucchini, onions, bay leaves, and celery. Sauté 10 to 15 minutes, or until onions are lightly browned. Spread vegetables over the sole, retaining the pan juices. Garnish the sole with the raisins and pine nuts. Add the vinegar and wine to the pan juices and hold over high heat until reduced to about half. Pour the liquid over the garnished sole and keep refrigerated for 24 to 48 hours.

Side Dishes

Pine-nut Corn Pudding

2 cups corn kernels
1 chopped green pepper
1 zucchini, chopped
2 tablespoons chopped, roasted pine nuts

Place ingredients in blender and blend thoroughly. Place ingredients from blender in a medium-sized pan, bring to a boil, and simmer until thick. Serve hot.

Rice Albuquerque

1½ cups rice
1 tablespoon Tabasco sauce (or to taste)
1 tablespoon butter
½ cup pine nuts

Boil rice until done. Add Tabasco sauce and butter to rice. Sauté pine nuts in butter and add to the rice mixture. Serve warm.

Pilaf Athenian

1 cup finely chopped onion
6 tablespoons butter
1 cup white rice
1 medium clove garlic, finely minced
2 tablespoons chopped parsley
2½ cups chicken broth
¼ cup raisins
½ teaspoon salt
¼ teaspoon pepper
⅓ cup pine nuts

Sauté the garlic and onion in 4 tablespoons butter until lightly browned. Place the sautéed onion and garlic, rice, parsley, chicken broth, raisins, salt, and pepper in a 2-quart casserole. Mix well. Bake in covered casserole at 375° for ½ hour, or until broth is absorbed. Brown pine nuts in the remaining 2 tablespoons butter and blend with the rice.

Pine-nut Pilaf

2 cups rice
4 cups chicken broth
1 cup pine nuts
½ cup raisins
1 cinnamon stick
2 cloves, whole
⅛ teaspoon crushed saffron

Cook all ingredients (except pine nuts) in chicken broth, until done. Add nuts and serve warm.

Cookies

Neapolitan Fruit Cookies

½ cup butter
2 cups sugar
2 teaspoons vanilla
6 eggs
5 cups flour
½ teaspoon salt
1 tablespoon baking powder
⅔ cup candied fruit mixed with ⅔ cup pine nuts

Cream butter and sugar until light and fluffy. Add vanilla and eggs. Combine flour, salt, and baking powder; gradually add to the egg, butter, and sugar mixture. Chill the dough for 1 hour. Divide the dough into four equal parts. Roll out each part on a floured board until 12 inches long and 8 inches wide. Sprinkle the dough with ⅓ cup of nuts and candied fruit. Roll the dough tightly to make a loaf. Place the rolls on a baking sheet. Bake in a 375° oven for about 30 minutes or until golden.

After removing the rolls from the oven, allow them to cool for 8 minutes. Cut in diagonal slices about ½-inch thick. Place the slices on a baking sheet and bake in 350° oven for 15 minutes. Cool and store in airtight containers. Makes 5 to 6 dozen.

Fiesta Cookies

2 cups whole wheat flour
4 cups white flour

2 teaspoons baking powder
1 teaspoon salt
2 cups shortening
1½ cups granulated sugar
¾ cup water
1 cup pine nuts

Mix dry ingredients. In a separate bowl, blend shortening and sugar. Gradually add dry ingredients. Slowly add water until dough is smooth. Add pine nuts. Roll out on floured board about ½-inch thick. Cut into shapes and sprinkle with sugar and nutmeg. Bake in 375° oven for 10 to 12 minutes.

Lemon Drop Cookies

4 eggs
1½ cups sugar
½ teaspoon grated lemon rind
2½ cups flour
¼ teaspoon salt
¼ cup confectioner's sugar
1 cup pine nuts (if nuts are large, they should be chopped)

Place hot water in the lower part of a double boiler. Combine granulated sugar and eggs in the top of the boiler; beat until lukewarm. Remove from boiler and beat mixture until cool. Add lemon rind and fold in flour and salt. Place tablespoons of the mixture on an oiled cookie sheet. Cover with confectioner's sugar and nuts. Bake in 375° oven for 10 minutes. Makes about 2-dozen cookies.

Pine-nut cookies

1 cup butter
¼ cup confectioner's sugar
2 cups flour
1 teaspoon nutmeg
2 teaspoons vanilla
1 teaspoon cinnamon
1 tablespoon water
1 cup chopped pine nuts

Cream butter and sugar. Add the flour, 1 tablespoon water, vanilla, cinnamon, nutmeg, and nuts and mix well. Shape into small balls and place on cookie sheets. Bake at 325° for 15 to 20 minutes. Coat with confectioner's sugar while still warm. Makes 5 to 6 dozen.

Piñon Nut Balls

1 pound ground pine nuts
1 teaspoon vanilla
1 cup evaporated milk
3 cups powdered sugar

Grind pine nuts; mix with evaporated milk, vanilla, and powdered sugar. Make balls and roll in powdered sugar. Place on waxed paper and allow to stand until firm.

Breads and Cakes

Piñon Applesauce Fruit Cake

3 cups strained applesauce
1 cup shortening
2 cups sugar
4½ cups flour
4 teaspoons baking soda
1 teaspoon nutmeg
2½ teaspoons cinnamon
1 teaspoon salt
½ teaspoon cloves
1 pound dates
1 pound raisins
¼ pound pine nuts
¼ pound walnuts, chopped
¼ pound candied cherries
¼ pound candied pineapple

Boil together for 5 minutes the sugar, shortening, and applesauce. Let stand overnight. Dredge fruit, walnuts, and pine nuts with flour, soda, spices, and salt which have been sifted together. Mix all ingredients together. Bake in pans lined with waxed paper at 250° until an inserted toothpick comes out clean. A 1½-pound bread loaf takes 3 hours to bake. Fill pans two-thirds full.

Pine-nut Banana Bread

½ cup butter
1 cup brown sugar
2 eggs
2 cups flour
½ teaspoon salt
½ teaspoon soda
1½ cups mashed bananas
1 cup pine nuts

After creaming the butter and sugar, add the mashed bananas and the eggs and blend thoroughly. Combine flour, salt, soda, and pine nuts and blend into the mixture. Pour into a buttered loaf pan and bake at 350° for 45 minutes to 1 hour.

Pine-nut Pumpkin Bread

1 cup brown sugar
½ cup granulated sugar
1 cup canned pumpkin
½ cup salad oil
2 eggs, unbeaten
2 cups flour
1 teaspoon baking soda
½ teaspoon salt
½ teaspoon nutmeg
½ teaspoon cinnamon
¼ teaspoon ginger
1 cup raisins
½ cup pine nuts
¼ cup water

Combine sugars, pumpkin, oil, and eggs. Beat until well blended. Sift together flour, salt, soda, and spices; add and mix well. Stir in raisins, nuts, and water. Spoon into well-oiled 9-inch loaf pan. Bake at 350° for 65 to 75 minutes.

Pine-nut Carrot Bread

2 cups flour
2 teaspoons soda
2 teaspoons cinnamon
½ teaspoon salt

¾ cup pine nuts
1 teaspoon vanilla
1½ cups sugar
2 cups grated carrots
3 eggs
1 cup raisins
¾ cup corn oil

Sift flour, soda, salt, and cinnamon. Make a well in dry ingredients in mixing bowl. Add other ingredients and blend. Bake in well-greased pan in 325 to 350° oven for 50 minutes.

Piñon Sponge Cake

1 pound pine nuts, finely chopped
1½ cups flour
1½ cups sugar
1 teaspoon cinnamon
rind of one lemon or orange
1 dozen eggs

Separate egg yolks and beat. Beat egg whites, adding the sugar gradually until egg whites are stiff. Blend in egg yolks, nuts, flour, lemon rind, and cinnamon. Pour into an ungreased tube pan and bake at 350° for 45 minutes.

Desserts

Tropical Dessert

16 ounces finely chopped pineapple
1⅓ cups sugar
¾ cup finely ground almonds
1 sponge cake
5 egg yolks
1 cinnamon stick
½ cup pine nuts
¼ cup raisins

Combine the almonds, egg yolks, sugar, chopped pineapple, and cinnamon. Cook, stirring constantly until mixture is clear. Remove and pour the mixture over the sponge cake. Sprinkle with raisins and pine nuts.

Pine-nut Torte (Robert West Howard)

Crust: 1 cup unsifted all-purpose flour
         2 tablespoons sugar
         6 tablespoons butter
         1 egg
         ¼ cup raspberry jam
Filling: 1 can (8 ounces) almond paste
         6 eggs, separated
         ¼ cup sugar
         ¼ cup all-purpose flour
         ¾ teaspoon baking power
         1 cup toasted pine nuts
         Sugar

For crust, mix sugar and flour in a small bowl. Add butter and rub with fingers until mixture is reduced to fine crumbs. Stir in egg thoroughly with fork, then press dough into a ball. Roll out to fit generously a 10-inch cake pan (or cheesecake pan) with removable bottom. Fit dough into pan, making a 1-inch-high rim. Spread jam over dough.

For filling, combine almond paste in a bowl with egg yolks, sugar, flour, and baking powder. Beat until smoothly blended. Whip egg whites until they hold short, distinct peaks. Beat about half the egg whites into the almond batter, then fold in remaining whites and a generous ½ cup of the pine nuts.

Pour batter into prepared crust. Scatter remaining pine nuts over the surface. Bake in a moderate oven (350°) for 35 minutes or until center feels firm when lightly touched. Cool slightly (or completely), remove pan rim, and sprinkle with sugar before cutting. Makes 10 to 12 servings.

Eggs Cortez

8 eggs
1¼ cups sugar
3 cloves
1 cinnamon stick
½ cup water
¼ cup rum, brandy, or sherry
⅓ cup pine nuts
¼ cup raisins

Beat egg yolks until thick and lemon colored. Pour eggs into a buttered dish, set the casserole dish in a pan of hot water, and bake at 350° for 30 minutes, or until eggs are puffy.

Syrup: Combine sugar, cloves, and cinnamon stick with ½ cup water. Boil until the sugar dissolves. Remove the cloves and cinnamon stick. Add brandy, sherry, or rum.

After cutting the eggs into squares, allow them to soak in the hot syrup until cold, about 2 hours. Garnish with pine nuts and raisins.

Aztec Bread Pudding

8 ounces stale white bread
1¼ cups brown sugar
⅓ cup grated cheddar cheese
¾ cup margarine
6 tablespoons margarine
1 stick cinnamon
⅓ cup pine nuts

Break the bread into cubes and brown in margarine.

Syrup: Boil sugar and cinnamon stick in ½ cup water for 3 minutes. Lightly oil a medium-sized casserole dish. Place layers of cubed bread, syrup, cheese, margarine, and pine nuts. Repeat. Bake in a 350° oven until brown. Serve hot with heavy cream.

Backpackers' Friends

Piñon Pemmican

1 cup pine nuts
1 pound milk chocolate, or 12-oz. package of chocolate chips
½ cup grated coconut

Melt chocolate in a double boiler, add nuts and coconut, and pour into a plastic sandwich box lined with foil. Place in refrigerator and allow to harden. Can be carried in parka pocket or packsack as emergency ration or snack.

Granola

½ cup vegetable oil
½ cup honey
1 teaspoon vanilla

4 cups rolled oats
2 cups 40% bran flakes
½ cup sunflower seeds
¼ cup sesame seeds
1 cup raisins
1½ cups pine nuts
½ cup coconut

Heat oil, honey, and vanilla in a large saucepan. Remove pan from the heat and add remaining ingredients; mix well. Spread in a 9-inch by 13-inch pan lined with foil. Bake in a 350° oven for 15 to 20 minutes.

Miscellany

French Toast Zacatecas

1 cup sugar
½ cup water
1 coconut, shredded
1 loaf of bread (1 pound, 8 ounces)
3 large eggs
1 tablespoon flour
1 cup margarine
2¾ cups sugar
1 whole cinnamon stick
1 cup water
⅓ cup raisins
½ cup pine nuts, chopped

Place the cup of sugar in ½ cup water in a saucepan. Over medium heat, bring to a boil and boil for 3 minutes. Add the shredded coconut, and cook for about 15 minutes, or until the moisture is absorbed and the coconut is dry. Remove from heat and let mixture cool. Place the coconut paste between two slices of bread. Combine the eggs and flour and beat; dip both sides of sandwiches in the egg and fry in the margarine until light brown. Drain on paper towels.

Syrup: Combine 2¾ cups sugar, 1 cup water, and the cinnamon in a frying pan and boil for 5 minutes.

Simmer each of the sandwiches for a few minutes, turning when needed. Serve garnished with pine nuts and raisins. Pour syrup over the sandwiches.

Pine-nut Cakes

1½ cups whole wheat flour
2 teaspoons baking powder
2 tablespoons sugar
¾ cup water
½ cup ground pine nuts
½ teaspoon salt
2 tablespoons shortening

Add shortening to dry ingredients and pine nuts. Gradually add water and knead dough for about 5 minutes. Break off enough dough and roll to make a tortilla-sized cake about ⅛-inch thick. Cook on griddle until golden brown. Serve with homemade jam or preserves.

Notes

Notes to Chapter 1

Most of the general information on the piñon-juniper woodland is from Lanner (1975) and Randles (1949). Major sources on pines included Mirov (1967); Shaw (1914); Critchfield and Little (1966) on distribution areas; Martínez (1948) on piñons in Mexico; Little (1968), Lanner (1975), Bailey and Hawksworth (1979), and Robert (1978) on piñon taxonomy. Juniper data are from Lanner (1975), Martínez (1963), and Florin (1966).

The Mogollon Rim is the divide between waters flowing northward into the drainage of the Little Colorado River and those flowing southward into the drainage of the Salt and Gila Rivers. It forms a rough line of separation between the northern and southern halves of Arizona.

Piñon taxonomy is in some respects controversial because it deals with a complex group that is rapidly evolving and because piñon populations, widely distributed across sometimes inaccessible terrain, are often not well known. The nomenclature of piñons can therefore be expected to show its own evolution in the years ahead.

Notes to Chapter 2

Information on pine paleobotany is mostly from Mirov (1967). The Madro-Tertiary Geoflora and its migration northward from Mexico is discussed by Axelrod (1958). The sequence of climatic and geologic events during geological time is taken from Dorf (1969), Kurtén (1968), Dodson (1960), and Leopold and MacGinitie (1972).

The confusion engendered by Mexico's pines can be appreciated by a look at the taxonomic record. In 1855, a German nurseryman named Roezl visited the Valley of Mexico and described 82 new pine species there. In 1914, George Russell Shaw reduced the pines in all of Mexico to 18 species and 17 varieties. A few years later, Paul C. Standley recognized 28 species and 2 varieties of pine in Mexico. When Prof. Maximino Martínez published *Los Pinos Mexicanos* in 1948, there were 38 species, 18 varieties, and 9 forms. Little and Critchfield, writing in 1969, recognized a total of 35 species in all of Mexico. There is considerable disagreement about the correct status of several possible species, and it is not likely to be resolved without extensive study in field and laboratory.

The formation of piñon summer shoots (not to be confused with "Lammas growth") is discussed in Lanner (1976).

Notes to Chapter 3

Data on mutation frequency are from Stebbins (1971); the origin of a new species "all at once" by quantum speciation is from the model suggested by Grant (1971). The quotation from Bacon was used by Loren Eiseley in *The Man Who Saw Through Time.* Data on piñon fossils are from Knowlton (1901) and Axelrod (1939).

Haller (1962) has suggested that a single cylindrical *monophylla* needle is better adapted to arid conditions than a cluster of two or three needles because its smaller surface area would lessen the transpiration of moisture. But since transpirational loss is influenced by many other factors, like the number, structure, and behavior of stomates, as well as by characteristics of the needle tissue itself, this may be an oversimplification.

The nature of the single needle has been subject to controversy. The German botanist F. Thomas noted in 1864 that each needle had but one vascular bundle: thus, it was a bona fide needle. But the French paleobotanist Charles Bertrand claimed in 1874 that the supposed needle was a modified twig. In 1882, the eminent German botanist Eduard Strasburger sided with Thomas's view, and the twig hypothesis faded away. In 1885 Prof. J. S. Newberry started a minor controversy by suggesting that the solitary-leaved piñon was a "somewhat dwarfed and depauperate form" of *P. edulis,* due to the aridity of its habitat. He was immediately challenged by Joseph Dalton Hooker of the Royal Gardens at Kew, who countered that, far from *monophylla* being a "depauperate" *edulis* as "doubtfully suggested by the late Dr. Engelmann, and more recently insisted upon by Professor Newberry," the reverse was closer to the truth. Hooker interpreted the cylindrical needle as a pair of needles cohering to each other. In 1885, Dr. Maxwell T. Masters of the Royal Society attributed the single-needle habit to the obliteration of one of a pair of needles early in its development. This idea was lent support by Wilhelm Schneider in Germany in 1913 and by the American botanist C. C. Doak in 1935. So matters stood until 1973 when careful anatomical studies showed that there is no "obliteration" of a second needle in the fascicle, but merely the failure of a second needle to start development (Gabilo and Mogensen 1973).

Notes to Chapter 4

Natural hybridization is often successful in plants, unlike the situation among animals. A good treatment of the subject is presented by Stebbins (1950). The concept of introgression was formulated by Anderson (1949). The dispersion of tree pollens and other fine particles in the atmosphere is a fascinating subject that has not received the synthetic treatment it deserves. A likely mechanism by which heavy concentrations of pollen could be moved long distances is discussed in Lanner (1966). The natural hybridization of piñon pines is covered by Lanner (1974a, 1974b, 1975). Geological history of Arizona is from McKee et al. (1967).

Notes to Chapter 5

Information on the behavior of wood rats is from Hoffmeister (1971) and Shelford (1963). Data on the use of ancient middens as a source of macrofossils are from papers by Wells (1966), Van Devender and King (1971), Mead and Phillips (1976), and Lanner and Van Devender (1974); and conversations with Van Devender, Mead, Phillips, and Wells

The fine state of preservation of some midden fossils must be seen to be appreciated. Piñon needles up to 30,-000 years old may still show each microscopic stomate sharply etched into the needle surface, the stomatal cavities still holding the tiny plugs of wax that reduced water loss during the needle's life. Occasionally a swollen gall can be found at the base of a fossilized needle that, when pried open with fine dissecting instruments, yields the mummified corpse of a gall-midge larva. These are not fossils in which mineral matter has replaced the organic material, but objects whose original tissues have been preserved by suitable atmospheric conditions. They are extremely fragile and must be handled carefully.

Notes to Chapter 6

Data on mammals is taken mainly from Hoffmeister (1971). The definitive work on dwarf mistletoe is by

Hawksworth and Wiens (1972). Burdick (1961) has monographed the fascinating sawflies of the genus *Xyela*. The life history of the piñon spindle gall midge and information on its parasite are from a paper by Houseweart and Brewer (1972). One of the gall midges of singleleaf piñon was discovered by Lanner and the other by Brewer and Lanner in northwestern Utah's Grouse Creek Mountains in 1972. They have not, at this writing, been formally described or given names.

Notes to Chapter 7

The story of the piñon jay and its relationship to the piñon has been taken mainly from Balda and Bateman (1971); Ligon (1971, 1974); Ligon and Martin (1974); and Ligon and White (1974). Vander Wall and Balda (1977) have described the relationship between the piñon and Clark's nutcracker.

Some of the Shoshone called the piñon jay by the name Hai (rhymes with high). They never hastened to collect pine nuts before the jays got them because, after all, "the birds plant them." Apparently, the Indians were satisifed with the results of the birds' planting efforts, and no indication has been found that piñon trees were planted by Indians. When the question was raised with a Nevada Paiute, she asked, "What for? They grow all around." In the 1930s, C. A. Harwell, then naturalist at Yosemite National Park, investigated an isolated *monophylla* grove he found along an old Indian trail in Tiltill Valley. An aged Paiute woman he interviewed recalled that her people used the trail when moving from Mono Lake to summer camps in the Sierra. She suggested that children dropping nuts along the trail were the planters of the wild orchard (Harwell 1937).

Juniper trees are also seeded by birds, as is well known, but the mechanism is a relatively simple one. Fruit-eating birds, especially robins and Townsend's solitaires, are attracted to the colorful fleshy berries of the juniper and harvest them in large numbers. The hard seeds pass the intestine and are excreted randomly by the flying birds. It is curious that both major plants of the woodland—the piñon and the juniper—depend on birds for their establishment.

In order for jays to have acted as an agent in the early evolution of piñons, they must have been contemporaneous with the early trees. The piñon fossil record extends back to the Middle Miocene occurrence of *Pinus lindgreni* (Axelrod 1939) in southern California. The oldest record of a jay is the Upper Miocene occurrence of *Miocitta galbreathi* in Colorado (Brodkorb 1978). In a private communication, Dr. Brodkorb stated that *Miocitta* resembled the present-day piñon jay and Clark's nutcracker. Thus, despite the very restricted fossil record for piñon pines and corvids, we can place a piñon species and a jay similar to modern seed-caching jays in the Southwest at roughly the same time.

Notes to Chapters 8 and 9

A wealth of ethnobotanical information is in existence, much of it difficult to locate. The main sources consulted for these chapters are listed below by tribal name:

Navajo—Kluckhohn et al. 1971; Vestal 1952; Haile 1947; Elmore 1944; Babington 1950.

Hopi—Whiting 1939.

Pueblo—Lange 1939; Parsons 1925; Robbins et al. 1916; Underhill (n.d.).

Walapai—Kniffen et al. 1935; U.S. Senate 1936.

Coahuilla (Cahuilla)—Barrows 1900; Bean 1972.

Gosiute—Chamberlin 1911.

Panamint—Dutcher 1893.

Chumash—Grant 1965.

Northern Paiute—Wheat 1967; Muir 1894; Scott 1966; Steward 1933.

Tepehuan—Pennington 1969.
Apache—Terrell 1972; Reagan 1930.
Zuñi—Stevenson 1908.
Washo—Downs 1966.

Correspondence with National Park Service personnel throughout piñon country has disclosed the occurrence of piñon and juniper materials in numerous Southwestern archeological sites. At Chaco Canyon National Monument, New Mexico, piñon and juniper beams have been dated at 500 A.D. A house ruin dated at 1040 A.D. also had piñon timbers, and there were numerous seed coats of piñon in the house (Dutton 1938). Cave habitations in the Gila National Forest, New Mexico, had piñon and juniper seeds in floor deposits laid down from 300 B.C. to 1400 A.D. Materials of both species were abundant in Basketmaker III sites from 500 A.D. in Mesa Verde National Park, Colorado. At Bandelier National Monument, New Mexico, evidence shows that piñon and juniper materials were used daily in the lives of the poeple who lived there in the 12th Century; at Saltbush Pueblo, whole piñon cones have been found in the house ruins. Piñon and juniper wood were used in construction during the Pueblo III period of Kayenta Anasazi at Navajo National Monument, Arizona. Other evidence of such building materials has been found at El Morro National Monument, New Mexico (1225–1350 A.D.); Wide Reed Ruin, Arizona (1276 A.D.); Tuzigoot National Monument, Arizona (1125–1450 A.D.); and Tonto National Monument, Arizona (1250–1400 A.D.). The latter had piñon cones in habitations that were supported with piñon and juniper beams. Piñon resin was used as a dressing on arrow shafts, and juniper was used as a food (the berries) and as a tobacco substitute (the shredded bark smoked in cane cigarettes). Juniper bark torches have been found at Tonto, and also in the prehistoric salt mine near Montezuma Castle National Monument, Arizona, believed to have been in use from 1100 to 1450 A.D. Piñon wood has been found in Fremont sites dating from 900 A.D. at Capitol Reef National Monument, Utah, and in numerous undated habitations in Canyonlands National Park and Natural Bridges National Monument, Utah.

In many of these sites, as well as at others elsewhere in the Southwest, piñon timbers have been especially valuable in dating the ruins. Because piñon pine grows on semiarid sites, it is sensitive to year-to-year variations in rainfall. Years of heavy rainfall produce a wide annual ring of stem growth, and drought years produce extremely narrow annual rings. By correlating the pattern of wide and narrow rings in old living trees with those in beams cut during the lifetime of the live trees, it is possible to date the rings in the beams and to determine the year the beam was cut. Once the more recent beams are dated, older beams that overlap them in age can have their rings dated, and so on. Thus, dendrochronology has been an invaluable dating tool in Southwestern archeology, and the piñon pine has been its most important datable material.

Notes to Chapter 10

The development of pine cones is described in many botanical and forestry works and is well illustrated by Foster and Gifford (1974). The story of the relationship between the Shoshone of Nevada and the singleleaf piñon food resource has been elaborated in papers of David Hurst Thomas (1971, 1972, 1973); the Thomas extract in this chapter is from the first of these three sources.

White settlers learned very soon that the Indians had strong feelings about the trees that provided their food. The following extract from Myron Angel's *History of Nevada* provides amusing evidence:

> From a journal kept by Alf. Doten, who is present editor-in-chief of the Gold Hill *Daily News,* it appears that Numaga, on the thirteenth of October, 1863, met some of

the leading citizens of Como, in Lyon County, among whom was the journalist, and through his interpreter, uttered a formal protest against any further destruction of the pine nut groves. He said that his people depended upon the nuts from these trees for food; that the *"pine nut groves were the Indian's orchards,"* and they must not be destroyed by the whites. That they were welcome to the fallen or dead timber, but he should not permit a destruction of that portion which yielded food for his followers.

This warning was not heeded, and it was followed by the sudden and unexpected appearance upon the scene of numerous dusky forms, who with lowering looks so thoroughly frightened the wood-choppers, that they fled to Como and spread a war panic in the town.

Martial law was declared in Como by Martin, the Wizard; pickets were posted, and a courier dispatched to Fort Churchill for military assistance. That night, a lieutenant with twenty men galloped into the place and took charge of the besieged garrison. The next night every one "who prowled the mid-night darkness," were supposed to have the countersign or suffer a sudden calamity. Two citizens met "in the gloaming," and so scared each other that both forgot the password, and "turned loose" in the most approved style with their revolvers, each supposing he was having a struggle for life with, possibly, Numaga himself. The alarm was general and fearful to contemplate. A butcher, in his hurry to rush to the general defense from midnight massacre of the town, in his haste to get hold of it, accidentally fired off his gun, and then, as the aforesaid Alf. Doten, without the fear of God before his eyes, remarked, "Hell did pop." The next morning the Indians came into town to see what all the row was about.

The cyclic nature of cone crops has long vexed botanists and foresters. Regardless of what internal mechanism and environmental trigger might be necessary to produce a bumper crop, we might intuit that the boom-bust cycle serves some vital purpose. Otherwise, why would it have evolved in so many tree species? Forcella (1978), among others, has suggested the interesting possibility that these cycles have evolved as a defense against the destructive larvae of the cone moth *(Eucosma bobana)*. If cone crops were of constant size from year to year, cone moths would build up their populations and consistently decimate the annual crop. But if a large crop follows a poor one, the few moths emerging from the riddled cones of the previous year can place their eggs in only a small fraction of the current year's cones.

Notes to Chapter 11

The Shoshone story of the pine-nut tree's arrival in Nevada was related by Mr. Saggie Williams of Battle Mountain. The Washo explanation of the trees' short stature is adapted from the version given by Katherine Gehm (1970). Wallis (1936) recorded the Shumopovi tale of the picaresque misadventures of Coyote and Badger. The other stories are adapted from versions reported by Espinosa (1936) and Alvarado Cata (1956).

Notes to Chapter 12

Cabeza de Vaca's story is told in various reprints of his journal (e.g., Cabeza de Vaca 1936; Bandelier 1972), by Long (1941), and by Terrell (1962). What Cabeza de Vaca really said about the piñon was:

> Comían tunas y piñones; hay por aquella tierra pinos chicos, y las piñas de ellos son como huevos pequeños, mas los piñones son mejores que los de Castilla, porque tienen las cáscaras muy delgadas.

For reasons not at all clear, the Bandelier translation renders *"pinos chicos"* as "small trees of the sweet pine," which is how the passage is usually quoted. Hallenbeck (1940) reconstructs Cabeza de Vaca's trail and evaluates the several routes proposed by other historians. Escalante's journal was consulted in the Bolton version (1950).

Frémont's journal makes fascinating reading, but it should be remembered that it is not a field diary; it was written with the help of his talented wife, Jessie, after his return to Washington. Reference material for some of the other historical figures in this chapter is as follows: Ferris —Ferris (1940); Lieutenant Abert—Galvin (1966); Espejo —Hammond (1966); the Bartleson-Bidwell party—Lillard (1942) and Quaife (1928); Juan Cristobal—Loomis and Nasatir (1967); Coronado, Castañeda, and party—Winship (1896); Father Garcés—Coues (quoted in U.S. Senate 1936); and the Donner-Reed party—McGlashan (1940) and Thornton (1945).

Other Southwestern travellers, including the explorers Capt. L. Sitgreaves and Lts. Joseph C. Ives and A. W. Whipple in the 1850s, also commented on the piñons they encountered. Both Ives and Whipple noted the denseness of some of the woodland they passed through, as well as the use of piñon nuts for food by Indians and wildlife. Whipple's journal (1856) often mentions an absence of timber during the crossing of New Mexico. This does not indicate the absence of woodland, however, because by "timber" Whipple seems to have meant large trees like ponderosa pine and Douglas-fir.

Notes to Chapter 13

Some of the classical works on pines that mention species with edible nuts are Shaw (1914) and Gordon (1858). In addition to the North American pines with large edible nuts mentioned in chapter 13, there are several from other continents. These are Italian stone pine (*Pinus pinea*), Swiss stone pine (*P. cembra*), Siberian stone pine (*P. sibirica*), Japanese stone pine (*P. pumila*), Korean stone pine (*P. koraiensis*), and, from the Himalayas, Chilgoza pine (*P. gerardiana*). All are important in their local cultures and cuisines. The food quality of pine nuts has been reported by Little (1938), Botkin and Shires (1948), Smith

(1953), and, most recently, Watt and Merrill (1963). The data on amino acids and fatty acids of Colorado piñon and singleaf piñon resulted from laboratory analyses I had made by Albion Laboratories, Clearfield, Utah, and are published here for the first time. Yield information has been gleaned from Downs (1966), Kitson (1923), Howell (1941), Maule (1930), Randles (1949), Perry (1922), Phillips (1909), Steward (1933), and Vestal (1952).

A few years ago, I read in the Indian newspaper *Wassaja* that two young California children died in 1970 from eating raw pine nuts, which contain "oil of turpentine" and must be roasted to be made edible. When I wrote the reviewer, a Cahuilla named Costakik, to dispute the point, he answered that "at the age of 68, I have eaten more piñon nuts than you ever dreamed of" and they are poisonous unless cooked. Since then I have made it a point to ask long-time pine-nut fanciers if they ever heard of the "Costakik Effect." A New Mexican acquaintance of mine who "grew up" on piñons had a childhood friend who was apparently allergic to raw piñons. This is the only case I know of. A Paiute lady has told me that while raw pine nuts are not poisonous, Indians prefer to cook them, and whites prefer them raw.

Notes to Chapter 14

Frémont's correspondence with John Torrey is quoted from Jackson and Spence (1970) though none of Torrey's answers are reported. Since the Rodgers biography of Torrey (1942) also fails to report these answers, I assume that these letters (if they existed) were not preserved or have not been found. Wislizenus's memoir (1848) is the primary source of information on the travels of this interesting gentleman, who advocated, among other things, that the U.S. "indemnify itself" after the Mexican War by annexing New Mexico, Chihuahua, Sonora, and Alta and Baja California, thereby to enlarge the "area of freedom of mankind," to provide a railroad route from Laredo, Texas, to Guaymas on the Gulf of California, and to secure a defensible border. Zenas Leonard's journal has been edited by Ewers (1959).

In October 1849, sixteen years after Zenas Leonard's visit to Pilot Peak, Capt. Howard Stansbury visited the same mountain. He found a Shoshone winter village that had just been erected by "savages [who] had been in the neighborhood to collect the nuts of the pine-tree, called here piñon for food" (Stansbury 1853).

Reports of the newly discovered piñon pines are by Andresen and Beaman (1963), Rzedowski (1966), and Robert (1978).

Notes to Chapter 15

For an overview of the mining industry of Nevada see Paul (1963).

The story of wood and charcoal use in the Great Basin is based on the reports of John Ross Browne (1867, 1868, 1869); Lillard (1942); Angel (1881); Murbarger (1956); Curtis (1884); Rossiter Raymond (1872, 1873, 1875); Hulse (1965); Neal (1975); Townley (1972); Thomas (1971); and Harris and Mulcahy (1971). The history of the Italian charcoal burners is told in detail by Grazeola (1969) and Earl (1969).

The extent of deforestation can be estimated very roughly from mineral production records. During the period 1859–1880, minerals worth $450 million were extracted from Nevada mines. Using Eureka figures for the value per ton of bullion ($348) and the number of tons of ore needed to produce a ton of bullion (three and a quarter tons), and assuming thirty bushels of charcoal to smelt a ton of ore, I estimate charcoal consumed to be 126 million bushels. This is the output of between 400,000 and 525,-000 acres of piñon woodland. The inclusion of acres denuded to provide sites for mills and towns, cordwood and lumber for domestic uses, and ties and firewood for the railroads would probably raise the total area to three quarters of a million acres, about an eighth of Nevada's woodland area.

Different figures are given by Young and Budy (1979), who point out that enormous amounts of piñon and juniper wood were used for fencing, cooking, and construction at outlying ranches in Nevada. They also point out the severe consequences to the woodland of wildfires that raged during this historic period. Mrs. E. R. Chase of Wells, Nevada, conveyed a gloomy picture of woodland conditions to Franklin Hough in 1878:

> The range east of the Humboldt Range is covered on its upper surface with piñon pine, and its lower part with juniper. The former supplies all the country hereabout, and the towns along the railroad, with fuel, and it is nearly all the timber in the eastern portion of Nevada. It is rapidly disappearing under the demands of the neighboring towns.
>
> There have been no experiments in forest-planting. Various seeds planted came to nothing. We have nothing for fencing, and fuel is getting scarce. We have no shade-trees around our dwellings. Nothing has resulted from government or State bounties for tree-planting.

Amazingly little information is available on the enormous ecological effects that woodcutting has had on particular environments. Winters (1974) provides historical information on deforestation in Europe and the Middle East, but precise data are usually lacking. A shortly-after-the-fact estimate of woodcutting was made for the goldfields area of Western Australia in 1966. Wood was harvested there for use as firewood, mine timbers, and railroad ties, mostly during the early twentieth century. The estimate that 25 million tons of firewood were taken from land yielding 3 to 4 tons per acre works out to about 7 million acres denuded, assuming no second cuts to the same acreage (Chippendale 1973). Such impacts have

probably been commonplace in industrial areas throughout the world, even in modern times, but little is known
of their effects.

There are, however, many condemnations of charcoal
makers, like the following, taken from an early report on
Rocky Mountain national forests (Ensign 1888, p. 77):

> The charcoal burner is the most conscienceless violator of
> law that we have, cutting everything down to poles 2
> inches in diameter. He leaves behind him barrenness and
> desolation. The traffic in charcoal is so exhaustive upon
> the forests, and so injurious to the best interests of the
> State, that wherever permitted it should be done under a
> license only . . . There are no reasons why the charcoal
> burner should longer be allowed to prey upon the timber
> and young forest growth.

An especially poignant example of how the federal
government disrupted a native economy based largely on
piñon use is provided by the Hualapai (Hualpai, Walapai)
of northwest Arizona. Originally these people lived on
game, roots, and seeds. By the 1870s they had been relo-
cated to the Colorado River valley, where the government
attemped to make them corn planters. By 1879, decimated
by disease and disenchanted with the hot climate of the
river bottom, they left their reservation in a body and
returned to their native mountains. After President Arthur set their mountain home aside as a new reservation,
the Commissioner of Indian Affairs decided to make them
raisers of cattle. By 1898 the Hualapai reservation was
being grazed by thousands of cattle and horses belonging
to white trespassers. In 1924, Indian Commissioner
McDowell threatened that if the Hualapai failed "to measure up to the full realization of the plan to induce them
to become cattle raisers, then it might be well to dispose
of the tribal herd [and] lease the whole reservation to
white cattlemen" (U.S. Senate 1936). Within a few
decades, the dependence of the Hualapai on cattle apparently having been achieved, the U.S. Forest Service exper-

imented with various methods of killing the reservation's piñon and juniper trees in order to make more room for grass growth. Uprooting the trees with chains dragged behind crawler tractors was found to be cheaper and more thorough than the use of chemical poisons, but in open stands oil and propane burners were recommended to kill individual trees (Arnold et al. 1964).

Notes to Chapter 16

Most of chapter 16 is adapted from Lanner (1977), to which recourse can be made for more complete references.

The Forest Service's policy on woodland eradication is detailed in two environmental impact statements issued by the Intermountain Region in 1973–1974. These are listed in the bibliography under the entry, "Forest Service USDA." Actually, more chaining has been done in national forests of the Southwestern Region (Arizona and New Mexico). However, chaining in that region has greatly diminished and, it appears, will be replaced by a more rational system of woodland management. In contrast, the Intermountain Region still plans to chain 397,-000 acres of Utah and Nevada woodlands by the mid-1990s regardless of research results. Often, a good way to estimate the economic value of a land management program in the West is to see who does it. If private landowners found chaining economic, they would engage in it; they almost never do. It is the public lands that get chained, and lands on Indian reservations.

Concerns about soil erosion in piñon-juniper woodlands may be misleading range ecologists, because a dense tree canopy, though it may reduce undergrowth, does not necessarily expose the soil. Utah botanists have found that in relic areas of woodland protected from grazing by unusually rugged topography, the soil is covered by an almost unbroken "cryptogamic crust." This crust is made up of mosses, lichens, fungi, algae, and diatoms living on the soil surface in a complex community little known to science. The crust may be up to several inches thick, and is gray-green in color. It is tough enough to greatly reduce the transport of soil particles by wind or water, but fragile enough to crumble under the boots of man or his cattle's hooves. Perhaps range managers need to learn more about how the crust functions and how much abuse it can take.

The opposition of Nevada's Indians to BLM chaining programs is due to more than self-interest. As Gladys Williams, a Battle Mountain resident, explained, "It takes away not just *our* food, but the animals' too."

Bibliography

Alvarado Cata, Regina. 1956. Two stories from San Juan Pueblo. *Western Folklore* 15(2):106–109.

Anderson, Edgar. 1949. *Introgressive hybridization.* New York: Wiley.

Andresen, J. W., and Beaman, J. H. 1961. A new species of *Pinus* from Mexico. *J. Arnold Arbor.* 62(4):437–441.

Angel, Myron, ed. 1881. *History of Nevada, with illustrations and biographical sketches of its prominent men and pioneers.* Oakland, Calif.: Thompson & West.

Arnold, J. F.; Jameson, D. A.; and Reid, E. H. 1964. *The pinyon-juniper type of Arizona: effects of grazing, fire, and tree control.* USDA Forest Service Prod. Res. Rep. No. 84.

Axelrod, Daniel I. 1939. *A Miocene flora from the western border of the Mohave Desert.* Carnegie Inst. Wash. Publ. 516.

————. 1940. Late Tertiary floras of the Great Basin and border areas. *Torrey Bot. Club Bull.* 67:477–487.

————. 1958. Evolution of the Madro-Tertiary geoflora. *Bot. Rev.* 24:433–509.

Babington, S. H. 1950. *Navajos, gods, and tom-toms.* New York: Greenberg.

Bailey, D. K., and Hawksworth, F. G. 1979. Pinyons of the Chihuahuan Desert region. *Phytologia* 44(3):129–133.

Balda, Russell P., and Bateman, Gary C. 1971. Flocking and annual cycle of the piñon jay, *Gymnorhinus cyanocephalus. Condor* 73(3): 287–302.

Barger, Roland L., and Ffolliott, Peter F. 1972. *Physical characteristics and utilization of major woodland tree species in Arizona.* USDA Forest Service Res. Paper RM-83.

Barrows, David Prescott. 1900. *The ethno-botany of the Coahuilla Indians of Southern California.* Chicago: Univ. of Chicago Press.

Bean, Lowell John. 1972. *Mukat's people; the Cahuilla Indians of Southern California.* Berkeley: Univ. of Calif. Press.

Beebe, Lucius, and Clegg, Charles. 1956. *Legends of the Comstock Lode.* Stanford: Stanford Univ. Press.

Beidleman, R. G. 1953. The islands of pines. *Living Wilderness* 18(Autumn):7–10.

Bidwell, John. 1928. Echoes of the past about California. Edited by Milo Milton Quaife. Chicago: R. R. Donnelley.

Bolton, Herbert E. 1950. Pageant in the wilderness: the story of the Escalante Expedition to the Interior Basin, 1776, including the diary and itinerary of Father Escalante translated and annotated. *Utah Hist. Quar.* 18:1–265.

Botkin, B. A., ed. 1951. *A treasury of western folklore.* New York: Crown.

Botkin, C. W., and Shires, L. B. 1948. *The composition and value of piñon nuts.* New Mexico Agric. Exp. Sta. Bull. 344.

Brodkorb, Pierce. 1978. Catalogue of fossil birds, Part 5 (Passeriformes). *Bull. Florida State Mus. Biol.* 23(3):139–228.

Brown, R. W. 1934. *The recognizable species of the Green River flora.* USGS Professional Paper 185C:45–77.

Browne, John Ross. 1867. *Report upon the mineral resources of the states and territories west of the Rocky Mountains.* Washington: Gov. Printing Office.

———. 1868. *Report of J. Ross Browne on the mineral resources of the states and territories west of the Rocky Mountains.* Washington: Gov. Printing Office.

Burdick, Donald J. 1961. A taxonomic and biological study of the genus *Xyela* Dalman in North America. *Univ. Calif. Publ. Entomol.* 17(3):285–356.

Cabeza de Vaca, Alvar Núñez . 1932. *The narrative of Alvar Núñez Cabeza de Vaca.* Translated by Fanny Bandelier. Barre, Mass.: The Imprint Society.

———. 1936. *Naufragios y comentarios, con dos cartas.* Madrid: Espasa-Calpe S. A.

Chamberlin, Ralph W. 1911. *The ethno-botany of the Gosiute Indians of Utah.* Mem. Amer. Anthropological Assoc. vol. 11, pt. 5, pp. 329–405.

Chippendale, G. M. 1973. *Eucalypts of the western Australian goldfields.* Canberra: Austr. Govt. Publ. Serv.

Clemmer, R. O. 1974. Directed resistance to acculturation: a comparative study of the effects of non-Indian jurisdiction on Hopi and Western Shoshone communities. Ph.D. dissertation, Univ. of Illinois.

Critchfield, W. B., and Little, E. L., Jr. 1966. *Geographic distribution of the pines of the world.* USDA Forest Service Misc. Pub. 991.

Curtis, Joseph Story. 1884. *Silver-lead deposits of Eureka, Nevada.* USGS Monogr., vol. 8. Washington: Gov. Printing Office.

Dallimore, W., and Jackson, A. Bruce. 1961. *A handbook of Coniferae including Ginkgoaceae.* London: Edward Arnold.

DeVoto, Bernard. 1947. *Across the wide Missouri.* Boston: Houghton Mifflin.

Dodson, Edward O. 1960. *Evolution: process and product.* New York: Reinhold.

Dorf, Erling. 1969. Paleobotanical evidence of Mesozoic and Cenozoic climatic changes. *No. Amer. Paleontol. Conv. Proc.,* pt. D, pp. 323–346.

Douglas, J. Sholto, and de J. Hart, R. A. 1978. *Forest farming.* Emmaus, Pa.: Rodale Press.

Downs, James F. 1966. *The two worlds of the Washo, an Indian tribe of California and Nevada.* New York: Holt, Rinehart & Winston.

Dutcher, B. H. 1893. Piñon gathering among the Panamint Indians. *Amer. Anthropol.* 6:377–380.

Dutton, Bertha P. 1938. *Leyit Kin, a small house ruin, Chaco Canyon, New Mexico.* Albuquerque: Univ. of New Mexico Press.

Earl, Phillip I. 1969. Nevada's Italian war. *Nev. Hist. Soc. Quar.* 12(2): 47–87.

Eiseley, Loren. 1973. *The man who saw through time.* rev. ed. New York: Scribner.

Eisner, T.; Johnessee, J. S.; Carrel, J.; Hendry, L. B.; and Meinwald, J. 1974. Defensive use by an insect of a plant resin. *Science* 184:996–999.

Elmore, Francis H. 1944. *Ethnobotany of the Navajo.* Albuquerque: Univ. of New Mexico Press.

Ensign, Edgar T. 1888. *Report on the forest conditions of the Rocky Mountains.* USDA Forestry Division Bull. No. 2, p. 77.

Espinosa, Aurelio M. 1936. Pueblo Indian folk tales. *J. Amer. Folklore* 49:69–133.

FAO. 1968. *Survey of pine forests, Honduras.* United Nations Development Program. FAO/SF 26-Hon 50.

Ferris, W. A. 1940. *Life in the Rocky Mountains. A diary of wanderings on the sources of the rivers Missouri, Columbia, and Colorado from February 1830 to November 1835.* Edited by Paul C. Phillips. Denver: Old West Publ. Co.

Fife, Austin E. 1957. Pioneer Mormon remedies. *Western Folklore* 16(3): 153–162.

Florin, R. 1963. The distribution of conifer and taxad genera in time and space. *Acta Horti Berg.* 20(4):122–312.

Forbes, Jack D. 1967. *Nevada Indians Speak.* Reno: Univ. of Nevada Press.

Forcella, Frank. 1978. Irregularity of pinyon cone production and its relation to pinyon cone moth predation. *Madroño* 25:170–172.

Forest Service, USDA. 1973. *Pinyon-juniper chaining programs on National Forest lands in the state of Utah. Final environmental impact statement.* Intermountain Region, Ogden, Utah.

————. 1974. *Pinyon-juniper chaining programs on National Forest lands in the state of Nevada. Final environmental impact statement.* Intermountain Region, Ogden, Utah.

Foster, Adriance S., and Gifford, Ernest M., Jr. 1974. *Comparative morphology of vascular plants.* 2d ed. San Francisco: W. H. Freeman.

Frémont, John Charles. 1845. *Report of the exploring expedition to the Rocky Mountains in the year 1842, and to Oregon and North California in the years 1843–44.* Washington: Blair and Rives.

Gabilo, E. M., and Mogensen, H. L. 1973. Foliar initiation and fate of the dwarf-shoot apex in *Pinus monophylla. Amer. J. Bot.* 60:671–677.

Galvin, John, ed. 1966. *Western America in 1846–1847. The original travel diary of Lieutenant J. W. Abert.* San Francisco: John Howell Books.

Garcés, Francisco. 1900. *On the trail of a Spanish pioneer: the diary and itinerary of Francisco Garcés, 1775–1776.* 2 vols. Translated and edited by Elliott Coues. New York: F. P. Harper.

Gehm, Katherine. 1970. *Nevada's yesterdays.* Palmer Lake, Colo.: Filter Press.

Gerhard, Peter, and Gulick, Howard E. 1967. *Lower California guidebook.* Glendale, Calif.: Arthur H. Clark.

Gibson, George Rutledge. 1935. *Journal of a soldier under Kearny and Doniphan, 1846–1847.* Edited by Ralph P. Bieber. The Southwest Historical Series, vol. 3. Glendale, Calif.: Arthur H. Clark.

Grant, Campbell. 1965. *The rock paintings of the Chumash, a study of a California Indian culture.* Berkeley: Univ of Calif. Press.

Grant, Verne. 1971. *Plant speciation.* New York: Columbia Univ. Press.

Grazeola, Franklin. 1969. The charcoal burner's war of 1879: a study of the Italian immigrant in Nevada. Master's thesis, Univ. of Nevada.

Gunnerson, James H. 1969. *The Fremont culture, a study in culture dynamics on the northern Anasazi frontier.* Papers of the Peabody Mus. Arch. and Ethnol., vol. 59, no. 2. Cambridge, Mass.

Haile, Berard. 1947. *Prayer stick cutting in a five night Navaho ceremonial of the male branch of Shootingway.* Chicago: Univ. of Chicago Press.

Hallenbeck, Cleve. 1940. *Alvar Núñez Cabeza de Vaca. The journey and route of the first European to cross the continent of North America, 1534–1536.* Glendale, Calif.: Arthur H. Clark.

Haller, J. R. 1962. The role of 2-needle fascicles in the adaptation and evolution of ponderosa pine. *Brittonia* 17(4):354–382.

Hamilton, A. 1965. A matter of a pinyon. *Amer. Forests* 71:60–61.

Hammond, G. P., ed. 1966. *The rediscovery of New Mexico, 1580–1594.* Coronado Cuarto Centennial Publications 1540–1940, vol. 3. Albuquerque: Univ. of New Mexico Press.

Harper, K. T., and Alder, G. M. 1970. *The macroscopic plant remains of the deposits of Hogup Cave, Utah, and their paleoclimatic implications.* Univ. Utah Anthro. Papers, no. 93. pp. 215–240.

Harris, E. W., and Mulcahy, W. W., eds. 1971. The Yager journals: diary of a journey across the plains. *Nev. Hist. Soc. Quar.* 14(1): 27–54.

Harwell, C. A. 1937. Single-leaf pine in Yosemite. *Yosemite Nat. Notes* 16:1–3.

Hawksworth, Frank G., and Wiens, Delbert. 1972. *Biology and classification of dwarf mistletoes (Arceuthobium).* USDA Agric. Handbook No. 401.

Hepting, George H. 1971. *Diseases of forest and shade trees of the United States.* USDA Agric. Handbook No. 386.

Hoffman, A. F. 1921. The pinyon-juniper land problem. II. Plan for handling the pinyon-juniper type and discussion. *J. Forestry* 19:537–545.

Hoffmeister, Donald F. 1971. *Mammals of Grand Canyon.* Illustrated by James Gordon Irving. Urbana: Univ. of Illinois Press.

Hooker, J. D. 1886. *Pinus monophylla*—the nut pine of Nevada. *Gard. Chron.* 24:136.

Hough, Franklin B. 1878. *Report upon forestry.* Washington: Gov. Printing Office.

Houseweart, Mark W., and Brewer, J. W. 1972. Biology of a pinyon spindle gall midge (Diptera:Cecidomyiidae). *Ann. Entomol. Soc. of America* 65(2):331–336.

Howell, Joseph, Jr. 1941. Piñon and juniper woodlands of the southwest. *J. Forestry* 39:542–545.

Hulse, James W. 1965. *The Nevada adventure: a history.* Reno: Univ. of Nevada Press.

Ives, Joseph C. 1861. *Report upon the Colorado River of the West explored in 1857 and 1858 by Lieutenant Joseph C. Ives, Corps of Topographical Engineers, under the direction of the Office of Explorations and Surveys, A. A. Humphreys, Captain, Topographical Engineers, in Charge, by order of the Secretary of War.* 36th Cong., 1st Sess., Senate Doc. 90. Washington: Gov. Printing Office.

Jackson, D. and Spence, M. L. 1970. *The expeditions of John Charles*

Frémont. Vol. 1, travels from 1838 to 1844. Urbana: Univ. of Illinois Press.

Jameson, Donald A., and Reid, Elbert H. 1965. The pinyon-juniper type of Arizona. J. Range Mgmt., pp. 152–153.

Jeffers, D. S. 1921. The pinyon-juniper land problem. I. Should the pinyon-juniper lands be included in the National Forests? J. Forestry 19:534–537.

Jennings, Jesse D. 1968. Prehistory of North America. New York: McGraw-Hill.

Kitson, L. C. 1923. Piñon. Amer. Forests 29:158–159.

Kluckhohn, Clyde; Hill, W. W.; and Kluckhohn, Lucy Wales. 1971. Navaho material culture. Cambridge: Harvard Univ. Press, Belknap Press.

Kniffen, Fred; MacGregor, Gordon; McKennan, Robert; McKeel, Scudder; and Mook, Maurice. 1935. Walapai Ethnography. Mem. Amer. Anthropological Assoc. no. 42.

Knowlton, F. H. 1901. A fossil nut pine from Idaho. Torreya 1(10): 113–115.

Kurtén, Bjorn. 1968. The age of dinosaurs. New York: McGraw-Hill, World Univ. Library.

Lange, Charles H. 1959. Cochiti, a New Mexico pueblo, past and present. Austin: Univ. of Texas Press.

Lanner, R. M. 1966. Needed: a new approach to the study of pollen dispersion. Silvae Genetica 15:50–52.

———. 1974a. Natural hybridization between Pinus edulis and Pinus monophylla in the American Southwest. Silvae Genetica 23:108–116.

———. 1974b. A new pine from Baja California and the hybrid origin of Pinus quadrifolia. Southwest. Nat. 19:75–95.

———. 1975. Piñon pines and junipers of the southwestern woodlands. In Proc. Symposium on pinyon-juniper ecosystems. Logan: Utah State Univ.

———. 1976. Patterns of shoot development in Pinus and their relationship to growth potential. Chap. 12 in Tree Physiology and Yield Improvement. Edited by M. G. Cannell and F. T. Last. New York: Academic Press.

———. 1977. The eradication of pinyon-juniper woodland: has the program a legitimate purpose? Western Wildlands (Spring):12–17.

Lanner, R. M., and VanDevender, T. R. 1974. Morphology of pinyon pine needles from fossil packrat middens in Arizona. Forest Science 20(3):207–211.

Leonard, Zenas. 1959. Adventures of Zenas Leonard, fur trader. Edited by John C. Ewers. Norman: Univ. of Oklahoma Press.

Leopold, Estella B., and Macginities, Harry D. 1972. Development and affinities of Tertiary floras in the Rocky Mountains. In *Floristics and Paleofloristics of Asia and eastern North America.* Edited by A. Graham. Amsterdam: Elsevier.

Ligon, J. David. 1971. Late summer-autumnal breeding of the piñon jay in New Mexico. *Condor* 73(2):147–153.

————. 1974. Green cones of the piñon pine stimulate late summer breeding in the piñon jay. *Nature* 250(5461):80–82.

Ligon, J. David, and Martin, Dennis J. 1974. Piñon seed assessment by the piñon jay, *Gymnorhinus cyanocephalus. Animal Behavior* 22(2): 421–429.

Ligon, J. David, and White, James L. 1974. Molt and its timing in the piñon jay, *Gymnorhinus cyanocephalus. Condor* 76(3):274–287.

Lillard, Richard G. 1942. *Desert challenge: an interpretation of Nevada.* New York: Knopf.

Little, E. L., Jr. 1938. *Food analysis of pinyon nuts.* USDA Forest Service Southwest For. & Range Expt. Sta. Res. Note 48.

————. 1966. A new pinyon variety from Texas. *Wrightia* 3:181–187.

————. 1968. Two new pinyon varieties from Arizona. *Phytologia* 17:329–342.

Little, E. L., Jr., and Critchfield, W. B. 1969. *Subdivisions of the genus Pinus (Pines).* USDA Forest Service Misc. Pub. 1144. Washington: Gov. Printing Office.

Long, Haniel. 1941. *Piñon country.* New York: Duell, Sloan and Pearce.

Loomis, N. M., and Nasatir, A. P. 1967. *Pedro Vial and the roads to Santa Fe.* Norman: Univ. of Oklahoma Press.

Martin, Alexander C.; Zim, Herbert S.; and Nelson, Arnold L. 1951. *American Wildlife and Plants.* New York: McGraw-Hill.

Martin, Paul S., and Mehringer, Peter J., Jr. 1965. Pleistocene pollen analysis and biogeography of the southwest. In *The quaternary of the United States.* Edited by Herbert E. Wright, Jr., and D. G. Frey. Princeton: Princeton Univ. Press.

Martínez, Maximino. 1948. *Los Pinos Mexicanos.* 2d ed. México: Ediciones Botas.

————. 1963. *Las Pináceas Mexicanas.* 3d ed. México: Universidad Nac. Autónoma de México.

Maule, W. M. 1930. The lowly pinyon of poor Lo. *Amer. Forests* 36:770–772.

McGlashan, C. F. 1940. *History of the Donner party, a tragedy of the Sierra.* Stanford: Stanford Univ. Press.

McGregor, John C. 1965. *Southwestern archaeology.* 2d ed. Urbana: Univ. of Illinois Press.

McKee, E. D.; Wilson, R. F.; Breed, W. J.; and Breed, C. S., eds. 1967. *Evolution of the Colorado River in Arizona.* Flagstaff: Mus. of Northern Arizona.

Mead, J. I., and Phillips, A. M., III. 1976. Late Pleistocene fauna and Vulture Cave, Grand Canyon, Arizona. Manuscript report.

Meehan, T. 1885. *Pinus edulis* and *Pinus monophylla*. *Bull. Torrey Bot. Club* 12(8):81–82.

Miller, Fred H. 1921. Reclamation of grass lands by Utah juniper on the Tusayan National Forest, Arizona. *J. Forestry* 19:647–651.

Miller, Wick R. 1972. *Newe Natekwinappeh: Shoshoni stories and dictionary*. Univ. Utah Anthro. Papers, no. 94.

Mirov, N. T. 1967. *The genus Pinus*. New York: Ronald Press.

Moorhead, Max L. 1958. *New Mexico's Royal Road; trade and travel on the Chihuahua Trail*. Norman: Univ. of Oklahoma Press.

Muir, John. 1894. *The mountains of California*. Reprint. Garden City, New York: Doubleday Anchor, 1961.

Murbarger, Nell. 1956. *Ghosts of the Glory Trail*. Palm Desert, Calif.: Desert Printers.

Neal, Howard. 1975. Desert ghosts, Death Valley charcoal kilns. *Desert* Nov. 1975, pp. 14–15.

Newberry, J. S. 1885. The relations of *Pinus edulis* and *Pinus monophylla*. *Bull. Torrey Bot. Club*. 12(5):50.

———. 1886. *Pinus monophylla* and *Pinus edulis*. *Bull. Torrey Bot. Club* 13:183–185.

O'Bryan, Deric. 1950. *Excavations in Mesa Verde National Park, 1947–1948*. Medallion Papers, No. 39. Privately printed for Gila Pueblo, Globe, Arizona.

Paher, Stanley W. 1970. *Nevada ghost towns and mining camps*. Berkeley, Calif.: Howell-North Books.

Parsons, Elsie Clews. 1925. *The pueblo of Jemez*. New Haven: Yale Univ. Press.

Raul, Rodman Wilson. 1963. *Mining frontiers of the Far West, 1848–1880*. New York: Holt, Rinehart & Winston.

Pennington, Campbell W. 1969. *The Tepehuan of Chihuahua; their material culture*. Salt Lake City: Univ. of Utah Press.

Perry, Walter J. 1922. A word for the lowly piñon. *J. Forestry* 20:521–526.

Phillips, F. J. 1909. A study of pinyon pine. *Bot. Gaz.* 48:216–223.

Randles, Quincy. 1949. Pinyon-juniper in the Southwest. In *Trees, Yearbook of Agriculture*, USDA, pp. 342–347.

Raymond, Rossiter W. 1872. *Statistics of mines and mining in the states and territories west of the Rocky Mountains for the year 1870*. 42d Cong., 1st Sess., House Rep. Ex. Doc. No. 10. Washington: Gov. Printing Office.

———. 1873. *Silver and gold: an account of the mining and metallurgical industry of the United States*. New York: J. B. Ford.

———. 1875. *Statistics of mines and mining in the states and territories west of the Rocky Mountains, seventh annual report.* Washington: Gov. Printing Office.

Reagan, Albert B. 1930. *Notes on the Indians of the Fort Apache region.* Anthropological Papers Amer. Mus. Nat. Hist. vol. 31, pt. 5.

Robert, M.-F. 1978. Un nouveau pin pignon mexicain: *Pinus johannis. Adansonia,* ser. 2, 18(3):365–373.

Rodgers, Andrew Denny, III. 1942. *John Torrey, a story of North American botany.* Princeton: Princeton Univ. Press.

Robbins, Wilfred William; Harrington, John Peabody; and Freire-Marreco, Barbara. 1916. *Ethnobotany of the Tewa Indians.* Smithsonian Inst. Bur. Amer. Ethnology Bull. 55.

Roust, Norman Linnaeus. 1967. Preliminary examination of prehistoric human coprolites from four western Nevada caves. *Univ. Calif. Archeol. Surv. Rpts.* 70:49–88.

Rzedowski, J. 1964. Una especie nueva de pino piñonero del estado de Zacatecas (México). *Ciencia* 23:17–20.

Sanchez, Thomas. 1972. *Rabbit boss.* New York: Knopf.

Scott, Lalla. 1966. *Karnee: a Paiute narrative.* Repr. by arrange. with Univ. of Nevada Press. New York: Fawcett Premier Book, 1973.

Shaw, George Russell. 1914. *The genus Pinus.* Publ. Arnold Arboretum, no. 5. Cambridge: Riverside Press.

Shelford, Victor E. 1963. *The ecology of North America.* Urbana: Univ. of Illinois Press.

Simpson, James H. 1964. *Navaho expedition: journal of a military reconnaissance from Santa Fe, New Mexico, to the Navaho country made in 1849.* Edited by Frank McNitt. Norman: Univ. of Oklahoma Press.

Sloane, Eric. 1965. *A reverence for wood.* Reprint. New York: Ballantine Books, 1973.

Smith, J. Russell. 1950. *Tree crops, a permanent agriculture.* New York: Devin-Adair.

Spencer, R. F.; Jennings, J. D.; et al. 1965. *The native Americans.* New York: Harper & Row.

Stansbury, Howard. 1853. *Exploration and survey of the valley of the Great Salt Lake of Utah, including a reconnoissance of a new route through the Rocky Mountains.* Senate Exec. Doc. No. 3. Washington: Robert Armstrong.

Stebbins, G. Ledyard. 1950. *Variation and evolution in plants.* New York: Columbia Univ. Press.

———. 1971. *Processes of organic evolution.* 2d ed. Englewood Cliffs, New Jersey: Prentice-Hall.

Stevenson, A. H.; James, L. F.; and Call, J. W. 1972. Pine-needle (*Pinus ponderosa*) induced abortion in range cattle. *Cornell Vet.* 42:519–524.

Stevenson, Matilda Coxe. 1908. Ethnobotany of the Zuñi Indians. *Ann. Rep. Bur. Amer. Ethnol.* 30:35–102.

Steward, Julian H. 1933. Ethnography of the Owens Valley Paiute. *Univ. Calif. Publ. Amer. Arch. Ethnol.* 33(3):233–350.

Terrell, John Upton. 1962. *Journey into darkness.* New York: Morrow.

———. 1972. *Apache chronicle.* New York: World Publishing.

Theisen, A. A.; Knox, E. G.; and Mann, F. L. 1978. *Feasibility of introducing food crops better adapted to environmental stress.* Rept. prep. for National Science Foundation. Washington: Gov. Printing Office.

Thomas, David Hurst. 1971. Historic and prehistoric land-use patterns in the Reese River Valley. *Nev. Hist. Soc. Quar.* 14(4):3–9.

———. 1972. Western Shoshone ecology: settlement patterns and beyond. In Great Basin Cultural Ecology, a Symposium. Edited by D. D. Fowler. Desert Res. Inst. Publ. Soc. Sci., no. 8. Reno, Nevada.

———. 1973. An empirical test of Steward's model of Great Basin settlement patterns. *American Antiquity* 38:155–176.

Thornton, J. Quinn. 1945. *The California tragedy.* Calif. Centennial edition. Oakland, Calif.: Biobooks.

Toulouse, Joseph H., Jr. 1949. *The mission of San Gregorio de Abo; a report on the excavation and repair of a seventeenth-century New Mexico mission.* Monogr. Sch. Amer. Res., no. 13. Albuquerque: Univ. of New Mexico Press.

Townley, John M. 1972. The Delamar boom: development of a small one-company mining district in the Great Basin. *Nev. Hist. Soc. Quar.* 15(1):3–19.

Underhill, Ruth. n.d. *Workaday life of the Pueblos.* Indian Life and Customs, no. 4. Bur. Ind. Affairs.

United State Senate. 1936. *Walapai Papers. Historical reports, documents, and extracts relating to the Walapai Indians of Arizona.* 74th Cong., 2d Sess., U.S. Senate Doc. No. 273. Washington: Gov. Printing Office.

VanDevender, T. R., and King, J. E. 1971. Late Pleistocene vegetational records in western Arizona. *J. Ariz. Acad. Sci.* 6:240–244.

VanderWall, Stephen B., and Balda, Russell P. 1977. Coadaptations of the Clark's nutcracker and the piñon pine for efficient seed harvest and dispersal. *Ecological Monogr.* 47(1):89–111.

Vestal, Paul A. 1952. *Ethnobotany of the Ramah Navaho.* Papers of the Peabody Mus. of Amer. Arch. and Ethnology, vol. 40, no. 4. Cambridge, Mass.

Wallis, Wilson D. 1936. Folk tales from Shumopovi, Second Mesa. *J. Amer. Folklore* 49:1–68.

Watt, Bernice K., and Merrill, Annabel L. 1963. *Composition of Foods.* USDA Agric. Handbook No. 8.

Weber, W. A. 1965. Plant geography in the Southern Rockies. In *The Quaternary of the United States.* Edited by Herbert E. Wright, Jr., and D. G. Frey. Princeton: Princeton Univ. Press.

Wells, P. V. 1966. Late Pleistocene vegetation and degree of pluvial climatic change in the Chihuahuan Desert. *Science* (1953):970–975.

Wheat, Margaret M. 1967. *Survival arts of the primitive Paiutes.* Reno: Univ. of Nevada Press.

Wheeler, Lt. George Montague. 1875. *Preliminary report upon a reconnaissance through southern and southwestern Nevada made in 1869 by 1st Lt. George M. Wheeler.* Washington: Gov. Printing Office.

Whipple, Lt. A. W. 1856. *Report upon the route near the thirty-fifth parallel. Report of explorations and surveys to ascertain the most practicable and economical route for a railroad from the Mississippi River to the Pacific Ocean, made under the direction of the Secretary of War in 1853–4.* 32d Cong., 2d Sess., Senate Ex. Doc. No. 78. Washington: Beverly Tucker.

Whiting, Alfred F. 1939. *Ethnobotany of the Hopi.* Mus. of Northern Ariz. Bull. 15.

Wilde, N. A. J. 1974. Charcoal burning in Wyre Forest. *Quar. J. Forestry* 48:303–315.

Winship, George Parker. 1896. The Coronado expedition, 1540–1542. *Ann. Rpt. Bur. Ethnol.,* pt. 1 (1892–1893), pp. 329–613.

Winters, Robert K. 1974. *The forest and man.* New York: Vantage Press.

Wislizenus, Adolph. 1848. *Memoirs of a tour to northern Mexico, connected with Col. Doniphan's expedition in 1846 and 1847 by A. Wislizenus, M.D.* Washington: Tippin and Streeper.

Young, James A., and Budy, Jerry D. 1979. Historical use of Nevada's pinyon-juniper woodlands. *J. Forest Hist.* 23(3):112–121.

Index

198   INDEX

Blister rust: piñon, 38; white pine, 38
BLM, 149; chaining of woodland by, 133, 136, 138, 140
Blue crow. See Jay, piñon
Blue Crow (mythical character), 82
Bradshaw Mountains, 27
Brewer, J. W., 40
Brodkorb, Pierce, 173
Bronowski, Jacob, 81
Browne, John Ross, 118
Bureau of Indian Affairs, estimate of 1960 pine-nut harvest by, 104
Bureau of Land Management. See BLM
Burro Canyon, 43

Cabeza de Vaca, Alvar Núñez, 88–89, 112; account of piñon by, 89, 177; route taken by, 89, 177; survival of, 89
Cahuilla Indians, 68
California, 3, 4, 8, 21, 22, 25, 50, 70, 91, 94, 96, 100, 109, 111, 142, 149, 173, 179
California, Gulf of, 88
Camino Real, 103
Canyonlands National Park, 27, 175
Capitol Reef National Park, 27, 175
Carbonari, 122, 124, 125, 129
Carbon dating of midden contents, 31–32
Carson Sink, 75
Castañeda (Coronado's chronicler), description of woodland by, 90
Castile, pine nuts of, 89, 91
Cedar City, Utah, 26

Central Arizona Uplift, 27
Cerro Potosí, 7, 115
Chaco Canyon National Monument, 174
Chaining: acreage cleared, 133; economics of, 136–37; effects on archeological resources, 139; effects on forage production, 136; effects on Indians, 140; effects on soil erosion, 137; effects on wildlife, 137–38; how done, 132; on Hualapai Indian Reservation, 182–83; purpose of, 133; reaction of Indians to, 184; results of, 136–40.
Charcoal manufacture: Condemnation of, 182; effect on piñon-juniper woodland of, 125–28; importance of in Nevada, 180–81; process of, 120–22
Chase, Mrs. E. R., 181
Chihuahua (Mex. state), 5, 89, 179; Mexican piñon nuts sold in, 100
Chihuahua, Ciudad, 113
Chihuahuan Desert, 31
Child of the Water, 63
Chinese laborers, 122, 128
Chipmunk, cliff, 36
Chipmunk, Uinta, 36
Chumash Indians, use of pine nuts as food by, 70
Cibola, 90
Climate, Pleistocene, 33–34
Cochiti, 66
Colorado, 4, 9, 16, 56, 91, 131, 132, 138, 142, 149, 174
Colorado Plateau, 1, 11, 19, 27, 58, 65, 75
Colorado River, 22, 27, 31, 92, 182
Columbia Plateau, 21
Comstock Lode, 118